WALKING

in

WISDOM

How to Access the Mind of Christ

and Make Good Decisions

Greg Mohr

Cover by Catalyst Media
Text Layout by Covenant Communication Solutions

ISBN: 978-0-578-91768-9

Published by Greg Mohr Ministries

P.O. Box 7702
Woodland Park, CO 80863

Acknowledgments

First, I want to thank John Osteen, Kenneth Hagin, Bob Nichols, Jack Hayford, Andrew Wommack, Paul Milligan, and Billy Epperhart for modeling the principles of wisdom and leadership that I have applied in my life and refer to in this book. Each of these men of God has imparted much truth, love, faith, and wisdom to me. I am eternally grateful.

Second, I want to thank Bill and Becky Caldwell for paying for the cost of publishing this book. Thanks so much for your friendship and for believing in our ministry. Your reward for this investment in our lives and ministry is great!

Finally, I want to thank my beautiful wife, Janice, for her undying commitment to me. It has demonstrated God's love and wisdom to me in so many practical ways; I love doing life with you, sweetheart! I dedicate this book to you and each of our children and grandchildren. I believe the principles shared in this book are the legacy we are passing to each member of our family as well as the scores of disciples we have been privileged to build relationship with in the past forty-plus years of ministry.

Endorsements

In over forty-five years of ministry, I have observed a consistent problem. Many Christians make hasty, ill-advised decisions in life, some with devastating consequences. Most of the time, these bad decisions are justified by invoking the mantra "God told me." But they are just thinly disguised excuses for being emotionally driven. Walking in wisdom and accessing the mind of Christ takes effort and a level of discipline that many Christians do not apply to themselves.

Walking in Wisdom is a roadmap, a must-read for anyone wanting to make wise, godly decisions in life. God has given Greg an amazing ability to present biblical principles clearly and show their application through real-life examples. I have been blessed to call Greg Mohr my pastor since 1986, and for twenty-four years of that time, serve together in the same church in North Texas (where I witnessed several of the examples given in this book). *Walking in Wisdom* and its author Greg Mohr are great gifts to the body of Christ. You will be blessed.

Paul Milligan
Chairman of the Board of Solaris Hospice
Director of the Business School at Charis Bible College
Former CEO of Andrew Wommack Ministries
Wake Forest, North Carolina

Greg Mohr has written another powerful and practical book! *Walking in Wisdom* helps us recognize, receive, and apply godly wisdom. Too often Christians let emotions or a distorted sense of spirituality make their decisions, sometimes resulting in hurtful consequences. This book can help alleviate that, teaching you to discern and apply godly wisdom throughout your life.

Sarah Bowling
Author and Speaker
Co-host of *Today with Marilyn and Sarah*
Founder of Saving Moses
Denver, Colorado

If there was ever a time when people needed wisdom and discernment, it is now! With confusion and chaos running rampant, Greg Mohr's newest book will help you walk in divine wisdom. Drawing from Scripture and decades of life experience, Greg unpacks principles that will help you make great life-decisions and enjoy the light of God's Word on your journey.

Tony Cooke
Bible Teacher and Author
Tulsa, Oklahoma

In the challenging times we are facing, we need a voice of clarity and wisdom. Greg understands that. He understands the times and season in which we are living and offers valuable insight on what we need to do in his new book, *Walking in Wisdom*. Wisdom is the principal thing, and this book will assist in guiding us toward it.

Duane Sheriff
Senior Pastor of Victory Life Church
Durant, Oklahoma

Greg Mohr has a unique perspective on God's Word, having pastored for many years, directed a Bible college, and traveled extensively around the world. He has a wealth of knowledge and experience to draw from, and it is evident in every project he does. His newest book, *Walking in Wisdom*, is no exception. You'll be enriched and enlightened as you read and learn to walk in the wisdom of God to avoid making costly and unnecessary mistakes.

Greg Fritz
Founder and President of Greg Fritz Ministries
Tulsa, Oklahoma

In his book, *Walking in Wisdom*, Pastor Greg reveals what God's wisdom is, where it is found, how to receive it, and then how implement it. This book is filled with sound biblical instruction and many practical examples on how to walk in wisdom in different areas of life. This book is a treasure for anyone seeking to grow in their relationship with the Lord, but especially those starting into adulthood.

Rick McFarland
Senior Pastor of River Rock Church
Colorado Springs, Colorado

Greg Mohr is a man of great wisdom and a trusted friend. His presentation of the subject of wisdom will be life changing for you. I highly recommend this inspired book.

Barry Bennett
Senior Instructor, Charis Bible College
Monument, Colorado

Christians are often too quick to make decisions, attributing their lack of critical thinking to "moving with the Holy Spirit." This is a problem. God, the source of all wisdom and knowledge, gives us the tools we need—including the Holy Spirit—to access His wisdom. I am happy to endorse my dear friend and colleague Greg Mohr's book, *Walking in Wisdom*. It is an encouraging and timely resource for understanding how to follow the Spirit and connect with the mind of Christ.

Billy Epperhart
CEO of Andrew Wommack Ministries
Woodland Park, Colorado

I love attending conferences where Greg Mohr is speaking; he is one of my favorite teachers. His new book, *Walking in Wisdom*, does not disappoint. It reflects one of his greatest life lessons: No man is an island. In this book, Greg brings out the importance of getting your spiritual wisdom from God's Word, the Holy Spirit, and the sound counsel of those you trust. How can you go wrong with that? Enjoy the book.

Pastor Bob Yandian
Founder and President of Bob Yandian Ministries
Tulsa, Oklahoma

My friend Greg Mohr's new book, *Walking in Wisdom*, is an overflow of his own hunger for God and His Word. I've been privileged to receive of God's wisdom through Greg, and know that as you read *Walking in Wisdom*, you too will have the opportunity to grow in God's wisdom and grace.

Scott Hinkle
Evangelist
Dallas, Texas

Table of Contents

Foreword

Greg Mohr's latest book, *Walking in Wisdom*, is a must read! Greg has served as Dean of Education and Director of Charis Bible College in Woodland Park, Colorado, for many years. His wisdom is sought out by leaders and ministers worldwide, and his books and teachings have blessed countless believers. This book will be no different.

In 1 Corinthians 2:7, the Apostle Paul speaks of the hidden wisdom of God: *"But we speak the wisdom of God in a mystery, even the hidden wisdom, which God ordained before the world unto our glory."* This wisdom is not hidden from us but is hidden for us. God gives us wisdom as believers, but it is up to us to learn how to walk it out. In these troubled times, our nation desperately needs men and women who walk in the wisdom of God. It is the key to breakthrough in this nation and in every area of our lives.

Greg Mohr is a man to learn from. He has sought out the wisdom of God, and for twenty-seven years, I have watched him walk in that wisdom as a gifted teacher, preacher, pastor, husband, father, and grandfather. I encourage you to read Greg's new book, *Walking in Wisdom*. But don't just read it; believe it and learn to walk it out. As you do, you will see and experience supernatural breakthroughs in your own life.

Dr. Bob Nichols
Founder and Pastor of Calvary Cathedral International
Fort Worth, Texas

Introduction

Our lives are the sum of the decisions we make, but sadly, not all those decisions are made using God's wisdom. Each of us can attest to the hurt and pain caused by bad choices, but it doesn't have to be that way. God's Word reveals His wisdom, and it is readily available to all who seek. The wisest man who ever lived said, "*Wisdom is the principal thing; therefore, get wisdom*" (Proverbs 4:7). That same man also said, "*Wisdom strengtheneth the wise more than ten mighty men which are in the city*" (Ecclesiastes 7:19). Wisdom is power. And in Proverbs chapter eight, Solomon says that wisdom is crying out from the rooftops and from every street corner. It's hidden in plain sight but only discernible to people who see and hear with their hearts.

I've known Greg and Janice Mohr for over three decades. Having ministered in their church dozens of times, I've seen God-given wisdom operate through them to establish a thriving community of believers that truly produced good fruit. And for the last ten years, it has been my privilege and honor to have them work alongside me as the directors of Charis Bible College and now directors of ARMI (the Association of Related Ministries International).

Greg has acquired God's wisdom and uses it constantly in his dealings with those the Lord has put in his care. I've personally seen him step in and resolve problems with a wisdom that certainly isn't common or natural. I would love to have a hundred like him working with me! Greg is anointed in this area, and I believe he has been inspired to write this book and share this wisdom with you.

The price of wisdom is far above rubies (Proverbs 3:13-15). This book and the truths it reveal are priceless. I believe you will be inspired, challenged, and enriched as Greg shares over forty years of mining wisdom from God's Word with you. Get ready to be blessed and equipped to flow in a greater depth of God's wisdom. It truly will change your life.

Andrew Wommack
President and Founder of Andrew Wommack Ministries and
Charis Bible College
Woodland Park, Colorado

Preface

I remember that day as if it were yesterday, even though I was only ten years old at the time. It was a beautiful summer day in June, and my mom had given me permission to spend the day with my best friend, Mike. Our plans included swimming at the public pool, getting hot dogs at the baseball field concession stand, and watching two teams in our league play before our game later in the day.

I walked to Mike's house and found a note on the door that said he had gone with his mom to pick up some things at the store. The note asked me to wait on the porch until they returned. It seemed like they were gone for a long time. While I waited, I found myself looking toward the beautiful blue sky and talking to God. I wasn't yet born again, but I believed there was a God. I still remember what I prayed: "God, there has to be more to life than just swimming, hot dogs, and baseball." Though I loved all three, God put it in my heart to realize there were higher priorities in life. I went on to pray, "God, show me why I am here, and show me how to live."

My parents had divorced two years earlier, and I felt lost without my dad around. I didn't have anyone to teach me how to play baseball, and though I loved the game, I wasn't very good in the fundamentals. I lacked confidence in most areas of my life and wanted desperately for someone to help me toward the path of success. I believe that void led me to pray. I know God heard me and has since answered that prayer in significant ways. Looking back on that event, I am thankful my friend and his mom were late returning that day. It gave me time to express my heart and reach out to God. And I have never regretted it.

Even though I was not saved at the time, that prayer opened the door for me to communicate my heart to the Lord. In that moment, God put a desire in my heart to have my own family that would stay together. But with no role model, I had to admit I did not know how to be a good husband or parent. Thus began a quest for wisdom throughout my teen years and beyond.

I finally heard the Gospel and was born again on Easter Sunday 1973. Since receiving the Lord, I have realized that Jesus and His Word are the only true sources of wisdom. As I have walked with the Lord and studied His Word, I have discovered several essential keys to walking in wisdom and accessing the mind of Christ. These keys have helped me make good decisions in life and resulted in the answer to the prayer I prayed as a ten-year-old boy. The goal of this book is to impart that knowledge to you. Each chapter contains a different scriptural principle I have learned and applied in my life. I have seen them produce wisdom, success, and good decision-making in myself and others, and I pray and speak that same result over you.

Chapter 1

The Value of Wisdom

The goal and vision for my life and ministry is to help people grow in wisdom, maturity, and grace. I received that vision through the following verse describing Jesus' life:

> *And Jesus increased in wisdom and stature, and in favor with God and men.*
>
> Luke 2:52

The Greek word here for "*favor*" is *charis,* which is also translated as "grace" in many places in the Bible. The word "*stature*" includes the concept of maturity. But what is wisdom? The Word of God tells us, "*Wisdom is the principal thing*" (Prov. 4:7). Yet, without a thorough understanding of this concept, how can we measure our growth and increase in it? While I do not pretend to have the final word on any subject, I do want to share with you what the Lord has revealed to me about the definition of wisdom.

Wisdom is the grace to prioritize and correctly apply knowledge for the greatest common good. It is the ability to know what to do, to know what principle to apply in a situation that will produce life, good fruit, and leave people better off. It is the grace to help us keep the main thing the main thing. A. R. Bernard, author and pastor of Christian Cultural Center in Brooklyn, New York, said, "This generation is information rich and wisdom poor." That is a sad but true statement. We have never before seen a time when information is more available. This generation can access it at their fingertips. Yet we still see major dysfunction in families, hatred and violence in society, and animosity and division among the leaders of our nation. Information alone cannot resolve the problems we face. The answers to our problems are only discovered and resolved in God's wisdom.

To more fully understand this concept of wisdom, we must know the difference between wisdom, knowledge, and understanding. This is what the Lord revealed to me that has helped me personally walk in wisdom in my life. ***Knowledge is the accumulation of truth and facts. Understanding is the proper arrangement of truth and facts*** (so you know where you have filed it and can easily access it again). ***Wisdom is the proper application of truth and facts*** (so you apply the right principle of truth to the right person at the right time). One verse that confirms this revelation is found in the book of Proverbs, *"The tongue of the wise uses knowledge rightly"* (Prov. 15:2).

A wise person knows how to apply knowledge appropriately. Have you ever met someone with little tact? It seems they are always putting their foot in their mouth, saying the wrong thing, or maybe the right thing but at the wrong time. We have a close acquaintance known for his misspeaking. He is often condescending and talks over others' heads to impress people with his knowledge. He uses words and terms normal people—even educated people—don't typically use or understand. What he doesn't realize is *we cannot bless those we are trying to impress*. Why is that? Because impressing others is about us, not others. And when our focus is on ourselves rather than others, we can be certain that our thoughts, words, and actions are void of God's wisdom.

This individual says some of the rudest things to people in the name of honesty. I have witnessed people being so hurt by his brutal honesty, they needed to walk off and cry. I am not judging this individual or attributing bad intentions to him, but his harsh and rude statements, though at times factual, do not bless those with whom he shares. For example, he once told a female member of my family that she looked fat. He asked her what she had been doing that caused her to gain so much weight. It was embarrassing for us all but caused my family member to run to the bathroom for a good cry. I tried to communicate with this man how his attempt at honesty did not bless her. But he just brushed it off, saying that someone should tell her the truth. I guess he thought it was okay to appoint himself the bearer of such news. Another time, he told my wife she had gained more wrinkles since the last time he had seen her. My wife let him know he had a lot less hair since we had last seen him! That seemed to shut down his truthful but hurtful commentary.

The important thing to remember when sharing truth with people is that only truth spoken in love blesses others (Eph. 4:15). Also, "*a word in season*" encourages the weary (Isa. 50:4). If the truth can be spoken in love, then it can also be spoken outside of love. If we can speak a word in season to the weary, that implies it is also possible to speak a word "out of season" that fails to encourage the weary. As we will see later in this book, there is a strong connection between wisdom and love. Have you ever received a truth that wasn't shared in love, or a word not spoken in season or at the appropriate time? I am sure each of us can share examples of being on the receiving end of such wrong applications of truth. One thing is certain: that is not wisdom! It reminds me of the old Chinese proverb, "Do not attempt to remove a fly from your friend's forehead with a hatchet."

Wisdom is the appropriate application of knowledge.

In the simplest definition I can give, wisdom is the appropriate application of knowledge. But understanding the definition is not enough. We must value it correctly. Again, Proverbs tells us wisdom is the principal thing (Prov. 4:7). It is the priority. It is the first, the most important, the main thing in our lives. King Solomon, the wisest man in earth's history (prior to Jesus' birth), demonstrated his understanding of the priority and value of wisdom in an interaction he had with the Lord just after becoming king of Israel.

> *On that night God appeared to Solomon, and said to him, "Ask! What shall I give you?" And Solomon said to God: "You have shown great mercy to David my father, and have made me king in his place. Now, O LORD God, let Your promise to David my father be established, for You have made me king over a people like the dust of the earth*

in multitude. Now give me wisdom and knowledge, that I may go out and come in before this people; for who can judge this great people of Yours?" Then God said to Solomon: "Because this was in your heart, and you have not asked riches or wealth or honor or the life of your enemies, nor have you asked long life–but have asked wisdom and knowledge for yourself, that you may judge My people over whom I have made you king–wisdom and knowledge are granted to you; and I will give you riches and wealth and honor, such as none of the kings have had who were before you, nor shall any after you have the like."

2 Chronicles 1:7-12

Either God put this desire directly in Solomon's heart, or Solomon was taught this and had it modeled to him by his father David. In either case, Solomon knew what to ask for when presented with this question regarding the task of ruling over Israel. This is a great example to help us understand how to value and prioritize one biblical principle over another. While riches, honor, long life, and victory over our enemies are each important aspects of God's will for our lives, none of those principles trump wisdom. Just as in Solomon's life, when we seek God's wisdom and value it above what the world seeks, we will not only find wisdom, but all those other things will be added to us as well.

The Benefits of Wisdom

This reminds me of something Jesus shared with His disciples, mirroring this principle of valuing wisdom: *"But seek first the kingdom of God and His righteousness, and all these things shall be added to you*" (Matt. 6:33). If we will seek God's way of doing things, follow the pattern of His Word, and place value on the things He values, we will experience the benefits of wisdom. The ways of God's kingdom are not the same as the ways of the world. It is essential that each of us value His ways and His Word above other things we have been taught to value.

When we place the right value on wisdom, it will benefit us in many ways in this life and the life to come. Look with me at some of these benefits mentioned in Proverbs:

> *Do not forsake her, and she will preserve you; love her, and she will keep you. Wisdom is the principal thing; therefore get wisdom. And in all your getting, get understanding. Exalt her, and she will promote you; she will bring you honor, when you embrace her. She will place on your head an ornament of grace; a crown of glory she will deliver to you.*
>
> Proverbs 4:6-9

Look at the benefits this passage of Scripture declares come to us when we value wisdom appropriately:

1. She will keep, preserve, and protect you.
2. She will give you understanding.
3. She will promote you.
4. She will bring you honor.
5. She will keep you in grace.
6. She will crown you with God's glory (His manifest presence).

The following passage of Scripture from Proverbs 3 provides us with some additional insight into the significant benefits of wisdom.

> *Happy is the man who finds wisdom, and the man who gains understanding; for her proceeds are better than the profits of silver, and her gain than fine gold. She is more precious than rubies, and all the things you may desire cannot compare with her. Length of days is in her right hand, in her left hand riches and honor. Her ways are ways of pleasantness, and all her paths are peace. She is a tree of life to those who take hold of her, and happy are all who retain her.*
>
> Proverbs 3:13-18

This passage reveals that those who value wisdom receive:

1. Happiness
2. Length of days
3. Honor
4. Pleasantness
5. Peace
6. Life

These verses in Proverbs are not the only passages of Scripture that point to wisdom's great benefits. Ecclesiastes 9:16-18 tells us that wisdom is better than strength, might, and weapons of war. Proverbs 24:3 tells us that through wisdom, a house is built. Ecclesiastes 7:12 tells us that wisdom is our shelter. The Word reveals so many benefits of wisdom to us. I cannot take time in this one chapter to identify them all. But suffice it to say there is so much latent, untapped power in the form of wisdom stored up and ready to be released in the body of Christ (and in your life) that it has the potential to change the world!

There are deals yet to be made that will prosper you and bless the kingdom, the church, and others. There are "God ideas" and inventions that will bless the world and bring glory to God. There are new strategies to be developed that will increase productivity and excellence in the marketplace and church. There are answers and solutions to complex problems yet to be discovered. There are cures to age-old and new diseases yet to be found. There are new mediums of communication to be developed. There are relationships yet to be reconciled and restored. All of these things and more are waiting for the wisdom of God in you and me to be activated!

If you desire these results and benefits in your life, I encourage you to make wisdom the highest thing of value in your life. It is more valuable than riches or honor and will bring you all that you could ever desire in this life. After walking with the Lord for over forty years, I have discovered this to be true. God has been faithful to prove this to me, and He will do the same for you!

Chapter 2

Two Kinds of Wisdom

Before I begin sharing with you what God has taught me about how to access the wisdom of God, we need to focus on the reality that there are two kinds of wisdom. It is imperative that each of us be clear about this fact. There is the wisdom of God and the wisdom of the world, and we cannot afford to confuse one with the other.

As a young man searching for wisdom, I wanted to know how to live successfully to benefit others. However, in my search, I observed a number of leaders modeling to me something quite different than the wisdom of God. When I was eight years old, my dad abandoned my mom and his five children for another woman. I was the oldest child but had no idea how to help my mom with my three brothers and sister. Then I discovered that two different men attempted to have a romantic relationship with my mom while I was a teenager. And each of them was married! I also heard an adult family member, who I looked up to, and who had spent quality time with me and my siblings, speak of the opposite sex in demeaning and crude ways. He also cut off one of his close relatives for over a year because he didn't agree with some decision they made. And later, I even overheard him talking about being involved with underhanded business practices. What a disappointment! Another relative of mine—though kind, generous, and gracious to me—had a very quick temper. He often burst out in anger toward his family for little or no reason. This kept his family living in constant fear of him and caused some serious confusion for me. I was looking for someone in my life who modeled the wisdom of God, but most of what I experienced was not godly.

At least three passages of Scripture reference a distinction between the wisdom of God and the wisdom of the world. Let's look at the first passage found in First Corinthians 1.

> *For the message of the cross is foolishness to those who are perishing, but to us who are being saved it is the power of God. For it is written: "I will destroy the wisdom of the wise, and bring to nothing the understanding of the prudent." Where is the wise? Where is the scribe? Where is the disputer of this age? Has not God made foolish the wisdom of this world? For since, in the wisdom of God, the world through wisdom, did not know God, it pleased God through the foolishness of the message preached to save those who believe. For Jews request a sign, and Greeks seek after wisdom; but we preach Christ crucified, to the Jews a stumbling block and to the Greeks foolishness, but to those who are called,*

both Jews and Greeks, Christ the power of God and the wisdom of God. Because the foolishness of God is wiser than men, and the weakness of God is stronger than men.

1 Corinthians 1:18-25

Here, the Apostle Paul tells us the wisdom of the world is actually foolishness. He also declares that we cannot know God through the wisdom of this world. The psalmist says something similar in Psalm 53.

The fool has said in his heart, "There is no God."

Psalm 53:1

By comparing these two passages, we can understand why the wisdom of the world is so dangerous. It is deceptive. It sounds good, but it results in death. I was looking for wisdom as a young boy and teenager, but what I found did not manifest or reveal God to me at all. It was the wisdom of this world.

First Corinthians 1 reveals two primary enemies to the message of the cross and the wisdom of God:

- Jews – self-righteous Pharisees
- Greeks – all-knowing philosophers

The Jews trusted in their works and esteemed themselves better than others because they didn't violate the law. They lived better, less sinful lives and substituted their religious works for the wisdom of God. The Greeks, on the other hand, trusted in their human knowledge and learning. This caused them to esteem themselves better than others who did not have their knowledge. They substituted education for the wisdom of God. Paul tells us each of these positions is foolish. Each is in opposition to the wisdom of God and makes itself an enemy of the cross.

Because of the emphasis on grace in many churches today, I am not as concerned about the Pharisees who trust in their law-keeping and good works to make themselves right with God. I am much more concerned about the philosophers who exalt their own understanding above the cross. These individuals are actually trusting in the wisdom of this world rather than the wisdom of God, keeping themselves from an intimate relationship with Him.

Another passage of Scripture in Isaiah 5 also makes this distinction between the two kinds of wisdom:

> *Woe to those who call evil good, and good evil; who put darkness for light, and light for darkness; who put bitter for sweet, and sweet for bitter! Woe to those who are wise in their own eyes, and prudent in their own sight! ... Who justify the wicked for a bribe, and take away justice from the righteous man!*
>
> Isaiah 5:20-21, 23

I read these verses many times in the past, and though I knew they were true because they are from God's Word, I never thought I would see them become a reality in my lifetime. But today, we are seeing this happen before our eyes. Politicians and civil leaders vilify those who stand up for truth. Many deceived men and women are calling evil good and good evil, putting darkness for light and light for darkness. In today's culture, those who stand up for women's rights, including the right to abort or kill a baby in the womb, are hailed as heroes. These "heroes" say it is not our place to tell a woman what she can and cannot do with her body. But this "wisdom" is not the wisdom of God!

Now, I am not condemning or judging anyone who has chosen to have an abortion in the past, and neither does God. I am choosing to agree with the wisdom of God and what He says about a woman's right to abort her baby. The wisdom of the world says it is okay to abort or kill your baby. The wisdom of God says it is not. God hates hands that shed innocent blood (Prov. 6:16-17)! If you find yourself with an unplanned pregnancy, there are other options. Go to your family or to a pregnancy center. Go to a church in your area to receive support and help during your pregnancy. You might choose to give up your child for adoption. But whatever you do, I am appealing to you, do not act on the wisdom of the world. It is foolishness and will not produce life, peace, faith, or hope for you.

> I want to speak the wisdom of God to every person who claims to be pro-choice. There is one couple I am sure you are happy was pro-life—your parents!

If you have already had an abortion, there is forgiveness and mercy with God. I thank God for this redeeming truth. If you are born again, you will see your baby in heaven. But knowing and receiving that grace does not mean it is okay to change the truth — God's wisdom—in an attempt to remove your guilt. Only the blood of Jesus can do that when we believe in His sacrifice on the cross.

I want to speak the wisdom of God to every person who claims to be pro-choice. There is one couple I am sure you are happy was pro-life—your parents!

This is just one example of an issue where people are calling evil good and good evil, assigning light for darkness and darkness for light. Verse twenty-three of Isaiah 5 says that this same group of people who call evil good and good evil will take bribes from the wicked and condemn the righteous. We see politicians, CEOs of large corporations, and much of the media doing this very thing today. They are willing to justify evil causes and those who represent them in exchange for what serves their own interests, whether it benefits them financially or helps keep them in power. That is the wisdom of this world, not the wisdom of God.

First, they overlook evil. Then they permit evil by legalizing it. Then they promote and celebrate evil. And finally, they persecute those who still call it evil.

It is the church's responsibility as the salt of the earth and light of the world to stand up for truth and warn our friends, family, and neighbors of the folly of the world's wisdom. When we observe a government or people accepting the wisdom of this world as a substitute for the wisdom of God, moral decline is inevitable. In a moral decline, society follows these steps: First, they overlook evil. Then they permit evil by legalizing it. Then they promote and celebrate evil. And finally, they persecute those who still call it evil.

The following passage of Scripture compares the wisdom of the world and the wisdom of God very clearly.

> *Who is wise and understanding among you? Let him show by good conduct that his works are done in the meekness of wisdom. But if you have bitter envy and self-seeking in your hearts, do not boast and lie against the truth. This wisdom does not descend from above, but is earthly, sensual, demonic. For where envy and self-seeking exist, confusion and every evil thing are there. But the wisdom that is from above is first pure, then peaceable, gentle, willing to yield, full of mercy and good fruits, without partiality and without hypocrisy.*
>
> James 3:13-17

James details the specific character traits of each type of wisdom. The wisdom of the world is described here as a wisdom that does not descend from above. It is sensual, or self-gratifying, and demonic. The wisdom of God is pure and produces only good fruit. Let's look at each type of wisdom, its character traits, and some examples of it in operation.

Wisdom of the World

1. *Bitterness* – The meaning of the word is to be sharp, harsh, or angry. Remember my family member who was kind, generous, and gracious to me but at times harsh and angry toward his family? That type of behavior is not the wisdom of God. Whenever we yield to bitterness, harshness, and

outbursts of anger, tolerating this as acceptable behavior, we have—perhaps unconsciously and unintentionally—exchanged the wisdom of God for the wisdom of the world.

2. *Envy* – This means to desire what others have. It can include the desire to be someone else or have their possessions or position in life. It is the result of not trusting God to provide for you and promote you. One of the benefits of the wisdom of God is that God will promote us, honor us, and provide riches for us (Prov. 3-4). Because He promised this to us, we can trust Him to bring that to pass in our lives. One of the family members I shared about earlier had adopted unscrupulous, and in some cases, illegal, business practices to meet his needs. He was modeling the wisdom of this world rather than the wisdom of God.

3. *Self-seeking* – The concept here is yielding to selfish ambition, even in the name of following God-given goals or dreams. We are self-seeking when we put ourselves forward at the expense of others or without thinking about others. This is what my dad modeled for us in his pursuit of another woman. He did not consider how those actions would impact my mom or his five young children. This Greek word for "*self-seeking*" was used often before New Testament times to describe an individual's pursuit of political office by unfair means. There was no method too low that this

person would avoid if it helped him accomplish his goal to defeat his opponent and gain public office. This is definitely the wisdom of the world, and one of the traits we see in operation most often today. But the end doesn't justify the means with the wisdom of God! James goes on to describe self-seeking as boasting to exalt or promote yourself to someone else's hurt or injury and lying against the truth (calling good evil and evil good) in order to accomplish your desired end. Stooping to the lowest moral standard in order to fulfill your goal is the wisdom of the world in its highest expression.

4. *Earthly* – This simply means pertaining to the natural realm. It may be common sense, but earthly wisdom does not always line up with the Word of God. That is why we need to have knowledge of the Word to help us distinguish the wisdom of the world from the wisdom of God. For example, one common, traditional saying I was brought up with was, "God helps those who help themselves." That sounds good on the surface, but when you read the Word, you find that God has mercy on those who don't deserve it (Matthew 5:45). Galatians 6:2 tells us we are to bear one another's burdens to fulfill the law of Christ, which is selfless love. Scripture also tells us that he who has pity on the poor lends to the Lord and the Lord will repay him (Prov. 19:17). These verses debunk that traditional thought process of God's willingness to help only those

with the wherewithal and resources to improve their own situations, proving that is not the wisdom of God. There are many such "good old boy" sayings we were brought up with that we must check out with the Word of God before accepting them as the truth.

5. *Sensual* – This word comes from the Greek word that is translated "*soul*" in Scripture and means that which is governed by the soul, emotions, passion, and reason. One of the men who showed kindness toward and interest in me as a teenager was my best friend's dad. He took me to their family cabin a couple of times and included me in some of their family functions. I appreciated the attention and favor he gave me, but he also shared "wise" counsel with me and his son that wasn't godly. One of the points of counsel he shared was that "sex is the most powerful thing in the world." At the time, I didn't know the Word very well, but that statement struck me as questionable coming from a married adult man. I thought if you were married, those needs would be met in your wife and wouldn't control you as much as when you were single. Later I found out that he had made sexual advances toward my mom. And he was already married! I also discovered from the Word that God is all-powerful and that when we are born again, we received the fruit of the Spirit, which includes self-control (Matt. 6:13 and 26:64; Gal. 5:22-23). The wisdom of the world tried to convince me that

sex was the most powerful thing in the world, but the wisdom of God says God is all-powerful and we can control (have power over) our passions! It is important to note here that though people can be kind and favorable toward you, that doesn't automatically mean they speak from the wisdom of God.

6. *Demonic* – This means to resemble or proceed from an evil spirit; to be demon-like. My wife and I once ministered to a lady who was hearing voices. Those voices told her to curse people, hurt people, and do things that were obviously evil and wrong. We told her these voices were not from the Lord because God would never tell someone to curse or hurt others. She said she knew the voices were from the Lord because they spoke to her about a hurricane that would hit her hometown in south Texas, and it happened just like the voices said. We asked her to consider that the devil (who caused that hurricane) knew where he would cause it to make landfall. We told her she was being deceived by familiar spirits. She could have been set free that day but decided to continue listening to the voices.

We need to take time to examine the fruit of the wisdom and counsel we are hearing. If it is full of emotional drama, strife, confusion, and bad fruit, it is NOT the wisdom of God.

This was very sad to us, but we could not force her to be free. People have to want to be free. They have to realize that the wisdom of the world produces confusion and every evil work. We need to take time to examine the fruit of the wisdom and counsel we are hearing. If it is full of emotional drama, strife, confusion, and bad fruit, it is NOT the wisdom of God.

Wisdom of God

1. *Pure* – This word means clean, chaste, modest; and free from defilement. The wisdom of God is not rude, unclean, or dirty, but trash and gutter talk is common with the world. I started sharing jokes at the beginning of my messages many years ago because I saw the fruit of laughter drawing lost and carnal people's attention to listen to the Word of God. Many later received the Lord and became part of the family of God. Since that time, I have received hundreds of jokes from people all over the world. Some of them I clean up and share. Others are funny but impossible to clean up enough for me to share publicly. I set those aside as impure and assign them to the wisdom of the world.

2. *Peaceable* – This word refers to that which is pertaining to peace, as opposed to confusion, strife, fighting, and drama. Proverbs 3:17 tells us that *all* the paths of wisdom are peace, not just some of them. When we walk in the peace of God in our

hearts and attempt to walk in peace with men, we can be assured we are in the wisdom of God. When we are experiencing a lack of peace in our hearts and constant strife and contention with men, it is a sign we are walking in the wisdom of the world. After my parents divorced, my mom moved our family from Davenport, Iowa, to Houston, Texas, to be closer to her family. Someone she trusted gave her counsel that as the oldest son, I should be the one to help my mom correct my siblings— including spanking them with a belt. My mom attempted to institute that counsel by having me spank my brother Layne (the second oldest child in our family) when he had done something wrong. It only took one or two attempts to determine this was *not* the wisdom of God. It created strife, drama, and confusion in the family, as well as anger and animosity between my brother and myself.

3. *Gentle* – This word means moderate, patient, equitable, and fair. The definition includes the idea of "sweet reasonableness." When I think of this aspect of the wisdom of God, I think of my pastor, Bob Nichols. He has modeled for me and many others the example of being fair, equitable, and patient. He always displayed sweet reasonableness, even when bringing correction to someone. Remember, it is the wisdom of this world that is harsh, rude, angry, and bitter—not the wisdom of God.

4. ***Willing to yield*** – This is actually one Greek word translated into an English phrase. It means "easy to be entreated" or persuaded. It also means someone who easily obeys or is compliant. The Bible tells us the willing *and* obedient eat the good of the land, not just the obedient (Isa. 1:19). The wisdom of God is willing to submit to authority in our lives. We'll talk about this later, but we haven't begun to submit until we are willing to do what someone in authority asks of us that we don't want to do. The only exception to this is something that is clearly sin or a violation of God's Word.

5. ***Full of mercy and good fruits*** – Mercy means full of kindness, compassion, and goodwill toward others. Good fruits are good works that produce good results in people's lives. It is mercy, kindness, and goodness in operation that impacts people's lives in tangible ways. It is Jesus-with-skin-on manifesting His mercy, love, and kindness toward people. The wisdom of God will always produce good fruit! This aspect of God's wisdom brings people to repentance (Rom. 2:4).

6. ***Without partiality*** – This means impartial or without prejudice or bias. The wisdom of God does not make decisions with a predisposed bias or prejudice. It is fair and impartial. You can trust someone who is walking in the wisdom of God to be fair and impartial, to stand on the truth, refusing

to be swayed by lobbyists, finances, or personal preference. Unfortunately, this is often lacking in our judicial and political system today. Most of their decisions seem to be prejudiced toward party and social groups or biased for their own financial gain. This is the world's wisdom prophesied in Isaiah 5:23 that justifies the wicked and takes justice away from the righteous.

7. *Without hypocrisy* – This means to be truthful and sincere. Its literal meaning refers to someone who does not act like a stage player or theater actor. It also means undisguised, unmasked, and without pretense. The wisdom of God does not pretend to be one thing when it is really something else. You can trust it to be truthful, sincere, and unchanging. There is no "put on" with the wisdom of God. To walk without hypocrisy requires one to be secure in their identity in Christ and to walk in the fear of the Lord when considering others' opinions. The wisdom of this world, however, changes with the wind. Like a chameleon, it pretends to be something and believe something that doesn't offend the crowd. But the wisdom of God allows you to be yourself, secure in who you are— no pretense or put on necessary!

> The wisdom of God provides us with true, lasting answers to life's problems that really work, and it causes us to bear good fruit.

The wisdom of this world may provide temporary answers, but it will eventually end up disappointing us. It will always lead us toward dependence upon the world system, others, or ourselves. The wisdom of God provides us with true, lasting answers to life's problems that really work, and it causes us to bear good fruit. You can be confident in it and its ability to connect us with God and His Word—the true source of wisdom.

Chapter 3

Realize You Have His Wisdom

In the previous two chapters, we learned the definition and value of wisdom, the benefits of walking in wisdom, and the two kinds of wisdom. In the next several chapters, I want to share with you what God has taught me about walking in His wisdom on a daily basis. Have you ever wondered how to consistently access the wisdom of God and make good decisions? That's what I prayed for as a ten-year-old boy, and God has been faithful to reveal those things to me. He will do the same for you! Scripture declares that Jesus has already been made wisdom to us. Let's look at that verse in First Corinthians.

> *But of him are ye in Christ Jesus, who of God is made unto us wisdom, and righteousness, and sanctification, and redemption.*
>
> 1 Corinthians 1:30 KJV

According to this verse, one of the greatest kingdom resources—God's wisdom—has already been imparted to us.

When we received Christ into our lives, our spirits were made righteous and filled with health, peace, and provision. But not all believers walk in the benefits of Jesus' finished work on the cross. This is especially true when it comes to wisdom. Do you remember when you first received the revelation that you were made righteous in your spirit—independent of your good or bad works—because of the sacrifice of Jesus? The following verse, along with what we just read in First Corinthians, makes this truth very clear.

> *For He made Him who knew no sin to be sin for us, that we might become the righteousness of God in Him.*
>
> 2 Corinthians 5:21

This revelation came to me through a teaching I heard from Kenneth Hagin six years after I was born again. When I first heard I'd been made righteous, it was hard to believe. I knew myself too well. Up to that time, I had identified with my sins and shortcomings more than the truth of the Word. For several weeks after hearing this and reading and meditating on it from the Word of God, I was still saying to myself, "This can't possibly be true of you, Greg—someone else maybe, but certainly not you. You know the kind of thoughts you have had, the kind of life you have lived, and all the things you have done wrong. How could you be righteous?" Then, a few weeks later, this verse in 1 Corinthians was made alive to me: "*Awake to righteousness, and do not sin*" (1 Corinthians 15:34).

I finally saw it. God was telling me not to judge my position of righteousness by my mistakes and the shortcomings of my flesh.

I realized I could not overcome sin by focusing on sin and the flesh. He showed me the way to overcome sin was to "awaken to" the fact that I was already righteous in my spirit man. The more I focused on and agreed with what He said about me, the more I was able to walk in dominion over sin.

Do you remember when you first understood you were healed by the stripes Jesus bore 2,000 years ago? Do you remember when you understood that healing was already yours because of the finished work of the cross? That revelation came to my wife and me through the teachings of Kenneth and Gloria Copeland, Kenneth Hagin, and John Osteen. At the time, we were fighting a major health battle with our fifteen-month-old son, Michael. After hearing the Word on healing taught over and over again, we finally realized the same sacrifice that paid for the forgiveness of our sins also covered our sicknesses and pain. By His stripes, we were—past tense—healed (Isa. 53:4-5; I Pet. 2:24). It was not long after we received this revelation that Michael's health began to improve, and eventually, he experienced complete healing of an incurable, arthritic muscular condition.

I took the time to detail these examples of the revelation we received about healing and righteousness because the same thing that is true of healing and righteousness is true of wisdom in your life. First Corinthians says that Christ has—past tense—been made wisdom unto you and me! Notice that wisdom comes first in this verse, even before righteousness. In other words, if you can believe He has been made righteousness to you, you can believe

He has been made wisdom to you. And like every other benefit of the cross, wisdom is voice activated. To receive it, you must believe it, embrace it, and speak it.

> *For assuredly, I say to you, whoever says to this mountain, "Be removed and be cast into the sea," and does not doubt in his heart, but believes that those things he says will be done, he will have whatever he says.*
>
> Mark 11:23

When we see a benefit God has given us through the sacrifice of His Son on the cross, we must believe it, agree with it, and declare it before we will see it manifest in our lives. For example, it may be true that I am not feeling well or that I am experiencing pain in my body, but I know I am healed by the stripes of Jesus. I have to believe, embrace and declare that truth before I will experience its reality in my body and receive the benefits of the healing Christ provided 2,000 years ago.

Until you realize you already have His wisdom, it won't become a reality in your life.

The same thing is true about the benefit of wisdom. Until you realize you already have His wisdom, it won't become a reality in your life. Jesus has already been made unto you wisdom, but that doesn't automatically make it a reality in your life. It's not going to fall on you like ripe cherries off a tree. Proverbs says that death and life are in the power of your tongue (Prov. 18:21). You have a part to play in believing and declaring the benefit of wisdom for it to become part of your experience.

A passage of Scripture in James 1 has caused many Christians to approach their request for wisdom from a place of deficit rather than surplus. Let's take a closer look at those verses together.

> *If any of you lacks wisdom, let him ask of God, who gives to all liberally and without reproach, and it will be given to him. But let him ask in faith, with no doubting, for he who doubts is like a wave of the sea driven and tossed by the wind. For let not that man suppose that he will receive anything from the Lord.*
>
> James 1:5-7

When we read the word "*lacks*" in this passage, our minds automatically focus on not having enough. Then our natural response is to ask for it, but many unintentionally ask from a place of deficit. I know, because that's what I used to do. But notice that verse 6 tells us to ask in faith. How can we ask in faith if we are not sure we will receive our request? How can we ask in faith if we are not sure God has already provided it? We can only have faith for what we know God's grace has provided. In other words, we cannot ask in faith without knowing God has already deposited all the wisdom we will ever need in our spirits.

Instead of asking for wisdom from a place of deficit or lack, ask from a place of surplus. Ask like you are writing a check or using a debit card with more than enough in your account to cover that purchase.

So, instead of asking for wisdom from a place of deficit or lack, ask from a place of surplus. Ask like you are writing a check or using a debit card with more than enough in your account to cover that purchase. That is what James is challenging us to do when requesting wisdom. Ask in faith, knowing He has already been made unto you wisdom. God has already imparted all the wisdom you will ever need in your spirit man. I may lack wisdom in my mind, but when I ask and declare in faith that I already have all the wisdom I need, the wisdom in my spirit is released for my use. Though I may not know what to do in my natural mind, when I ask and confess that Jesus has already been made unto me wisdom, I am writing the check or using the debit card on what has already been deposited in my spiritual account, and it will be revealed to me! First John chapter 2 confirms this truth to us.

> *But you have an anointing from the Holy One, and you know all things.*
>
> 1 John 2:20

Where is it that we know all things? In our spirits. That's where His wisdom has been deposited in us. The "*Holy One*" in First John 2:20 is the Holy Spirit, who lives and dwells inside each of us who know the Lord. And according to Isaiah 11:2, He is the Spirit of wisdom, understanding, counsel, and might.

You and I have the mind of Christ (1 Cor. 2:16). Where is it that we have His mind and wisdom? In our spirits, the same place we know all things and have received His wisdom. We draw out that wisdom residing in our spirits by believing and declaring these truths. Understanding this has been a real game-changer for me when it comes to walking in wisdom in my life.

Several years ago, I transitioned from my role as pastor of a life-giving church in North Texas and began serving at Andrew Wommack Ministries and Charis Bible College. I started out as a staff instructor supporting the main campus and extension school campuses. After two years, they created a brand-new position in the Bible college and offered it to me. Though my prior experience was in business and pastoring, I became the Dean of Education at Charis Bible College in Colorado.

I was honored by the leadership's trust in me, but I had zero experience as a dean of a major Bible college. All I had was twenty-seven years of pastoring experience and two years of experience as a staff instructor and overseer of the third-year ministry school program. I didn't know what a dean of education did. But I leaned into this "deaning grace" (meaning I agreed with what God said about me having the mind of Christ and enough of God's wisdom to do the job well). I trusted the decision the leadership made after praying that God would reveal the best person for the role. And I believed that this position was something God had assigned for me. I actually was involved with writing my own job description for this new role! As a result of my understanding and application of this truth, I experienced tremendous favor and success in that role. We instituted many new initiatives and programs, and the school grew significantly during that time. Though I didn't initially feel adequate for the role, God came through. He was made unto me wisdom for "deaning."

The reality is that I have never felt completely adequate for any new role or assignment God has given me. In order to accomplish anything in my life He (or someone else in authority) asks of me, I have to draw on His adequacy.

Not that we are sufficient of ourselves to think of anything as from ourselves, but our sufficiency is from God.

2 Corinthians 3:5

One major aspect of His adequacy at work in our lives is His wisdom. That's what Paul means when he says, *"We have the mind of Christ"* (1 Cor. 2:16). Though each of us have the mind of Christ deposited in our spirits when we are born again, we must realize that and declare it in order to receive that wisdom in tangible ways.

Many Christians never get to first base in this area because they are praying and/or confessing for wisdom from a place of deficit. They don't see themselves as adequate. They don't believe they have all the wisdom they need to do something beyond their present skill set, education, or comfort zone. But agree with me, dear friend, this will not be the case with you after understanding this powerful revelation! Jesus has been made unto you wisdom. You have the mind of Christ. Believe that, embrace and declare that, and the wisdom deposited in you will be released to your mind and manifested in your life.

Chapter 4

Meditate on the Word

Have you ever planned a long trip or vacation, packed up the car, loaded up your family, and discovered you had not filled up with gas? Or worse than that, found you needed an oil change? Perhaps the tire pressure was low on your tires? Failing to prepare adequately for a long trip can be costly.

A few years ago, my wife and I, with one of our sons and his family, planned a winter vacation together at a ski resort in northern Colorado. We decided to take our SUV because it could seat seven, allowing both our families to ride together.

The week we were on vacation was one of the coldest in recent Colorado history. The temperatures were as low as minus 20 degrees Fahrenheit and never got above seven degrees during the daytime. Skiing was miserable. With strong wind and the bitterly cold temperatures, even sliding down the tubing hills for more than an hour was challenging. We spent most of our time inside in front of the fireplace, drinking coffee and hot chocolate, instead of out on the slopes as we had planned.

On the way home, we drove in blizzard-like conditions, and my washer fluid froze up. I'd failed to change out the normal fluid for the kind that could handle sub-zero temperatures. We had to make a dozen stops on the way home just to clear the windshield from all the built-up ice, and though we had fun together, I was not adequately prepared for a trip in those conditions.

The more you renew your mind with God's Word, the more you will walk in the wisdom of God.

Each of our lives, no matter the specific longevity, is like a long trip (in sometimes-adverse conditions) that only the Word of God can sufficiently prepare us for. God's Word gives us wisdom for living. It prepares us for the various conditions and circumstances we will face on our life's journey. And it keeps us safe, helping us live successfully.

> *Behold, You desire truth in the inward parts, and in*
> *the hidden part You will make me to know wisdom.*
>
> Psalm 51:6

God desires to find truth deposited in your heart that He can use to impart His wisdom to you. The more of His Word you have taken time to meditate on and plant in your soul—your mind, will, and emotions—the more of His mind in your spirit will be accessible and released to you. Or you could say, The more you renew your mind with God's Word, the more you will walk in the wisdom of God. Make no mistake about it: God's Word is the source of wisdom! Failure to meditate on and renew our minds with God's Word results in us defaulting to the wisdom of this world.

> *Let the Word of Christ dwell in you richly in all wisdom.*
>
> Colossians 3:16

God's Word dwelling richly in you and me releases wisdom and brings a multitude of benefits into our lives, not the least of which is the ability to access the mind of Christ to make good decisions. Your personal, intimate knowledge of and relationship with the Word of God is key to this becoming a reality in your life.

> *For the word of God is living and powerful, and sharper than any two-edged sword, piercing even to the division of soul and spirit, and of joints and marrow, and is a discerner of the thoughts and intents of the heart.*
>
> Hebrews 4:12

The Word of God is the only thing that can divide and distinguish the soul from the spirit. It reveals the things that are of the flesh (which includes the soul) and the things that are of the spirit. Whenever an idea comes to me and I am trying to distinguish whether it is a "good idea" or a "God idea," I am really asking if that idea is of the spirit (where God dwells) or just a part of the soul. The more time we spend in His Word, the clearer that distinction becomes. Spending time in God's Word gives God more opportunity to use His Word to speak to us.

Let me share a couple of examples of how this has worked in my wife's life and in mine. I was saved in 1973 and later filled with the Spirit in 1976. Until I was filled with the Spirit, the Bible was a dark book to me. I did not understand it. After being filled with the Spirit, I had an insatiable desire to know and understand God's Word. Proverbs chapter 1 bears this truth out:

> *Surely I will pour out my spirit on you; I will make my words known to you.*
>
> Proverbs 1:23

I spent a lot of time reading and meditating on the Word during this time and seeking God about His will for my life. Two months after receiving the baptism in the Holy Spirit, I went on a fishing trip to northern Canada with my grandfather, my dad, and one of my brothers. Though we did catch some large northern pike and several nice walleyes, I actually spent more time in the Word than I did fishing. One day, while I was fishing with my brother and reading in Luke chapter 1, two phrases from two different verses seemed to leap off the page and into my heart.

> *Just as those who from the beginning were eyewitnesses and **ministers of the word** delivered them to us.*
>
> Luke 1:2

> *He will also go before Him in the spirit and power of Elijah, to turn the hearts of the fathers to the children, and the disobedient to the wisdom of the just, **to make ready a people prepared for the Lord**.*
>
> Luke 1:17

I had been seeking the Lord for over two months about His plan for my life and those two phrases from two separate verses (the phrases listed in bold) seemed to clearly answer my prayers. It was as if God Himself got in the boat with me that day and said, "I have called you to be a minister of the Word to make ready a people prepared for the Lord."

You could read those verses one hundred times and never put those two phrases together as He did for me that day. Though I struggled with that call for a period of time because I had a very successful business and felt inadequate to stand in front of people and teach, I could not deny that God had spoken to me. He answered me through His Word that day, and His Word has certainly come to pass since that time.

After I graduated Bible college, my wife and I planted a church in Houston, Texas. We served as pastors there for over three years and later merged that church with another in the area at the Lord's direction. Eighteen months later, a church in North Texas reached out to us. They asked us to move there and pastor. I prayed about it and believed we were to move and take that church. When I shared the direction I was sensing from the Lord with my wife, she said she also needed to hear from God before making such a major move. I was fine with that and prayed that if taking that church was God's will, He would confirm it to her. A couple of days later, she came to me with the following Scripture verses that God used to speak to her about our moving to take this church.

> *He takes away the first that He may establish the second.*
>
> Hebrews 10:9

...That ye should be married to another...that we should bring forth fruit unto God.

Romans 7:4 KJV

Though the context for each of these verses has to do with the new covenant superseding the old covenant, the Lord used them to speak to my wife about moving and pastoring our second church. The verses confirmed to her that God was moving us from one body of believers to another and that He would establish the second church as greater than the first, allowing us to bear much fruit.

During the twenty-four years we were in North Texas, that church grew from 60 members to over 300 in a town of 5,000 people. Many sons and daughters in the faith were raised up there and went into ministry, other churches and ministries were birthed out of that church, and we made many kingdom relationships. Dear friends, God's Word is living. It can speak to us specifically regarding His direction for our lives.

Another application of Hebrews 4:12 and the Word imparting wisdom to us often manifests as a supernatural "knowing." There have been times I have been seeking God about His will or wisdom in a certain situation and, while reading the Word, I just know what to do. I didn't know what to do previously, and the context of what I'm reading may not have anything to do with my situation, but all of a sudden, I know. Somehow, God just downloads the answer when I'm focused on Him.

One instance when this occurred was in 2008 just before the housing market crashed. We had just sold our home without listing it and were looking for a replacement home. All the houses we liked were priced higher than the house we had just sold yet had the same amount of square footage. We found one house we liked that was similar to the size of our previous home but was selling for a higher price than what we sold our home for. Another we really liked seemed to be a good price for the neighborhood but was over 1,000 square feet larger than our previous home and cost $100,000 more. Then we found another home that cost less but also had less square footage. With the closing of our previous home less than a month away, we didn't have much time to make a decision. I was leaning toward buying the larger home, but my wife felt we should purchase the smaller home. While reading the Word one day, I suddenly knew she was right. The smaller home was the one for us.

Not long after this, the housing market crashed. When we sold that home in Texas in preparation for our move to Colorado in 2011, we only lost $7,500. Had we purchased the larger house I had been leaning toward, we would have lost $75,000! Even more amazing, when we purchased a home in Colorado, we gained significantly more equity than the $7,500 we lost on the sale of our house in Texas! It is amazing how the living Word of God can bring wisdom to us, save us money, and even help us make money! This reminds me of a verse in Psalm 103:

> *He made known His ways to Moses, His acts to the*
> *children of Israel.*
>
> Psalm 103:7

Moses knew God's ways, and you and I can too. In fact, we can know God's ways even more because we are born-again children of God. As we spend time meditating in His Word, we can see His ways, His motives, His heart, His purposes, and His wisdom, and walk accordingly. Paul says it like this:

> *That I may know Him and the power of His resurrection, and the fellowship of His sufferings, being conformed to His death.*
>
> Philippians 3:10

Recognizing His Voice

We can know God and His ways, my brothers and sisters! We can walk in wisdom and manifest Jesus through our lives. But knowing Him requires knowing Him through His Word. Jesus and His Word are one. ***Knowing God, His Word, His ways, and His character is a prerequisite to recognizing His voice and walking in wisdom.*** Because I know His Word, His ways, and His character:

- I know He is peace, not confusion.
- I know He gives me hope, not depression.
- I know He is patient, His voice is not impulsive or pushy, and He does not pressure me to make quick decisions.
- I know He brings me into freedom; He does not lead me into bondage.
- I know He is meek and humble, so His voice is not going to lead me to be prideful, angry, arrogant, or rude.
- I know He leads me with confidence, not guilt and condemnation.

Whenever I am sensing a leading from the Lord—whether through an impression in my mind or heart, the Scriptures coming alive to me, or any other means—I take the time to check out how that leading lines up with the following passages of Scripture:

Love suffers long and is kind; love does not envy; love does not parade itself, is not puffed up; does not behave rudely, does not seek its own, is not provoked, thinks no evil; does not rejoice in iniquity, but rejoices in the truth; bears all things, believes all things, hopes all things, endures all things. Love never fails.

1 Corinthians 13:4-8

But the fruit of the Spirit is love, joy, peace, longsuffering, kindness, goodness, faithfulness, gentleness, self-control.

Galatians 5:22-23

If what I think I am hearing fails to line up with these passages of Scripture on love and the fruit of the Spirit, I refuse to act on it. At a minimum, I seek counsel about what I'm hearing and do not attempt to push it through in my own strength. Remember Abraham's mistake of attempting to force God's promise of a son through Hagar rather than Sarah. That mistake resulted in Ishmael and is still causing problems for Isaac's seed today.

We forsake the wisdom of God when we place a greater value on the supernatural way God speaks than on His written Word.

There are far too many "Ishmaels" being birthed outside of God's wisdom in the church today, all because we don't know God's Word and haven't learned God's ways. We forsake the wisdom of God when we place a greater value on the supernatural way God speaks than on His written Word. I am not impressed with the way you heard from God (whether it is by an angel, an audible voice, a dream, a vision, a prophetic word, or an open or closed door). I have received direction from the Lord through each of those supernatural means at various times in my life. But they are not the norm! Depending on the Lord to speak supernaturally is immature. That is not the primary way He leads us. The primary way He leads us is through His Word, the still small voice, or a strong desire He plants in our hearts that will be accompanied by peace. And that leading will always line up with His written Word. Always remember that "Thus saith the Lord" never trumps "It is written." Peter, by inspiration of the Spirit, confirms this in the following passage:

> *And this voice which came from heaven we heard, when we were with him in the holy mount. We have also a more sure word of prophecy* [more sure than the audible voice of God]; *whereunto ye do well that ye take heed, as unto a light that shineth in a dark place, until the day dawn, and the day star arise in your hearts.*
>
> 2 Peter 1:18-19 KJV

Peter was recounting hearing the audible voice of God on the Mount of Transfiguration where he met with Jesus, Moses, and Elijah. Yet he declares in this passage of Scripture that we have a *"more sure word of prophecy"* than the audible voice of

God. We have the written Word of God. This is wisdom, friends. God's written Word is surer than His audible voice or any other supernatural means of communication. Because I have spent time reading, studying, and meditating on God's Word, when certain thoughts surface in my mind, I don't need to pray about them. I know the Word, and I can judge whether or not that thought is wisdom. Five things I know are never from God are:

1. Fear
2. Doubt
3. Confusion
4. Discouragement
5. Guilt/Condemnation

Whenever these thoughts or emotions attack my mind, I know immediately it is the devil and not God. I cast that thought or emotion down with the Word, saying, "It is written":

1. *For God has not given us a spirit of fear, but of power and of love and of a sound mind"* (2 Tim. 1:7).
2. *"But let him ask in faith, with no doubting"* (James 1:6).
3. *"For God is not the author of confusion but of peace"* (1 Cor. 14:33).
4. *"Be strong and of good courage"* (Josh. 1:6).
5. *"There is therefore now no condemnation to those who are in Christ Jesus"* (Rom. 8:1).

Anytime the enemy comes to us with thoughts or emotions of fear, doubt, confusion, discouragement, or guilt and condemnation, we must realize that he is a thief and a liar. He comes to steal, kill, and destroy (John 10:10). The very fact that he has come to steal something from you proves you've already got it! Let wisdom and faith rise in your hearts, my brothers and sisters. Fill your hearts and mind with the Word of God, and you will walk in a greater measure of wisdom, access the mind of Christ, and make good decisions in life.

Chapter 5

Walking in the Fear of the Lord

Do you remember a time in your walk with the Lord when you had to make a choice between following God and His Word and displeasing or losing favor with someone you love and respect? Those are challenging decisions each disciple of Jesus is called to make as they grow in and follow the Lord. The decisions we make to walk in the fear of the Lord or yield to the fear of man determine the degree of wisdom we access in our lives.

> *The fear of the LORD is the beginning of wisdom.*
> Psalm 111:10

The fear of the Lord is the beginning—the starting place—of wisdom in our lives. If you and I want to walk in wisdom, this is where we must start. We cannot even get off home base until we have become established in the fear of the Lord. Let me make something clear as we begin this chapter on walking in the fear of the Lord: The fear of the Lord is not being afraid or fearful of God; rather, it is choosing to place a higher value on God and His

Word than the thoughts, desires, and opinions of others. It is not possible to walk in and draw on the wisdom within us until the fear of the Lord becomes a higher priority to us than the fear or opinions of man.

One area I have had to apply this truth to is in the performing of marriage ceremonies. Because God's Word clearly says that marriage is to be between a man and a woman and "*only in the Lord,*" this is the only type of marriage ceremony I will perform (Mark 10:6-8 and 1 Cor. 7:39). I do not pass judgment on any other types of weddings, but because of the fear of the Lord, I will only perform a marriage ceremony between a man and a woman who I know are born again.

I have actually led several individuals to the Lord during premarital counseling. I simply ask each if they are willing to make Jesus the Lord of their marriage. Typically, they are willing so I let them know the only way for Jesus to be Lord of their marriage is for Him to first become Lord of their lives. This opens the door for me to dig deeper and find out if they are truly born again. If not, I give them the opportunity to receive the Lord right then. Not one person has rejected Jesus during this time. They are motivated for their marriage to be successful. If anyone should reject the Lord when I share Jesus with them, then I would not perform the ceremony. I know that marriage won't work without Jesus at the center.

There are a few additional conditions I require be met before committing to perform a marriage ceremony. The couple must commit to four or five sessions of premarital counseling, and they must have known each other at least six months. I made these conditions a requirement after observing some marriages fail early in my ministry. I performed their ceremonies without having the couple go through premarital counseling or when the couple only knew one another for a short time.

I have had to draw on God's grace to remain in the fear of the Lord over this issue. Some families became upset with me and left the church over my commitment to follow what God instructed me to do regarding performing wedding ceremonies. But I have chosen to walk in the fear of the Lord in this area rather than the fear of man. I let them know I am not against their relationship and suggest they go to a Justice of the Peace or another minister willing to perform their wedding, but I have to do what God has instructed me to do. By refusing to allow a church member's anger, threats, or decision to leave the church change my commitment to following the Lord in this area, the divorce rate among marriages I perform is very low. This has proven to be God's wisdom.

> Whenever we yield to the fear of man, it takes us out of the wisdom of God because flattery, control, manipulation, selfish ambition, and lies rule that relationship—not Jesus!

This is just one example among several I will share with you about the opportunities I have had to walk in the fear of the Lord. I haven't walked perfectly in the fear of the Lord, but I have learned that following God's instructions is much better than yielding to pressure from men. The fear of the Lord is the beginning of wisdom. Whenever we yield to the fear of man, it takes us out of the wisdom of God because flattery, control, manipulation, selfish ambition, and lies rule that relationship—not Jesus!

> *The fear of man brings a snare, but whoever trusts in the LORD shall be safe.*
>
> Proverbs 29:25

God's Word declares that yielding to the fear of man will ensnare us. It will bring us into bondage, limiting our potential and our ability to lead others. It will cost us wisdom and promotion and, eventually, the respect of men. Yielding to the fear of man is what cost Saul his kingdom and, ultimately, his life.

> *Then Saul said to Samuel, "I have sinned, for I have transgressed the commandment of the LORD and your words, because **I feared the people and obeyed their voice.**" ... But Samuel said to Saul, "I will not return with you, for you have rejected the word of the LORD, and the LORD has rejected you from being king over Israel."*
>
> 1 Samuel 15:24, 26

What a sad story. God called and anointed Saul, through the prophet Samuel, to lead Israel as their first king. He began his reign in humility but ended in pride because of the fear of man. Eventually, both he and his son were killed in battle, and David succeeded him as king. The Bible says God rejects prideful leadership. He rejects leaders trapped in the fear of man. But we can learn from Saul's failure. While it is appropriate to serve God's people, it is never appropriate to follow the crowd instead of obeying what God has instructed us to do as His representatives.

The fear of man also cost Eli his place of leadership as Israel's priest. Eli's sons did not honor God. They stole the people's offerings and slept with prostitutes in the tabernacle. Though Eli knew about their sin and asked them to stop, he refused to take action to restrain them. Refusing to correct his sons cost Eli his children, his legacy, and eventually, his own life.

> *Why do you kick at My sacrifice and My offering which I have commanded in My dwelling place, and* **honor your sons more than Me**, *to make yourselves fat with the best of all the offerings of Israel My people? Therefore the LORD God of Israel says: 'I said indeed that your house and the house of your father would walk before Me forever.' But now the LORD says: 'Far be it from Me; for those who honor Me I will honor, and those who despise Me shall be lightly esteemed.'*
>
> 1 Samuel 2:29-30

Later, Eli and his sons died on the same day. But it did not have to happen. That was not their intended ending. If Eli had stood up to his sons and removed them from their roles for a period of correction, this situation could have been redeemed. But the fear of the Lord was lacking in Eli's life and leadership. The Bible says that he honored his sons more than God.

Both of these stories (the story of Saul and of Eli) reveal the danger of yielding to the fear of man. The fear of man will take us out of God's will and plan for our lives, and cause us to lose our places in the kingdom. This is not the wisdom of God!

Our Journey Walking in the Fear of the Lord

In our walk with the Lord, my wife and I have found that following the leadership of the Holy Spirit and obeying the call of God on our lives has required us to disappoint some people from whom we desired approval. Let me share a few of those instances with you.

My wife was filled with the Spirit while praying on the phone with a *700 Club* counselor. I had fallen asleep watching the *700 Club* television program that evening and woke up hearing her praying in a language I had never heard before. I went back to sleep thinking it was a dream but, the next week, noticed a change in her. She seemed like a different person. She was filled with joy, greater affection toward me (definitely a benefit I appreciated!), and a peace I had not seen or experienced with her before. The next Sunday, to my surprise, she walked to the front of our 1,500-member Methodist church and shared about her new experience with the Holy Spirit.

"I have been singing the doxology all my life," she said. "Praise God from whom all blessings flow; praise Him all creatures here below; praise Him above, ye heavenly host; praise Father, Son, and Holy Ghost." Janice went on to testify, "Every time we got to the last part, I used to think to myself, 'Praise Father, Son, and Holy Who?' I didn't know anything about the Holy Spirit. But last week, I was filled with the Spirit and received a heavenly prayer language. I want all of my friends to know the Holy Spirit is real. He is really, really real!"

Though many of the church members seemed blessed by her testimony, the pastor told her to sit down. He later called her into his office and told her that if she had any more experiences with the Holy Spirit, she was to share it with him before sharing with anyone else. He also told her that she and I could no longer teach the four-year-olds class on Sunday mornings and that we would need to stop teaching the youth group on Sunday evenings.

We subsequently left that church, and my wife found a lively, Spirit-filled church with clapping, dancing, and the gifts of the Spirit in manifestation. People were regularly saved, healed, and set free during services there. It was the closest thing I had seen to the book of Acts, but it caused no small stir with our family.

Most of Janice's family members belonged to our old Methodist church, while most of my family did not attend church at all. Many thought we had joined a cult. We received letters, phone calls, and visits from several friends and family members who had never expressed any concern about our spiritual condition previously. Most of these contacts warned us of the dangers of the new church we had joined. But we were growing in the Word there. We saw the Bible come alive through the move of the Spirit, and we (and our new church family) were more in love with Jesus than we had ever experienced in a church setting before. Everything demonstrated there the pastor backed up with Scripture, so we continued to attend.

In order to receive the fullness of our newfound freedom in Christ and walk in the Spirit, we had to suffer persecution. We never regretted taking that step of walking in the fear of the Lord by following God's leadership. Leaving the old church and moving to a new, life-giving church proved to be wisdom for us. Our real journey with Jesus began with that step.

Around that same period of time, I ran a wholesale florist business in Houston, Texas. The wholesale portion of my flower sales did not require me to charge state or city sales tax, but another portion of my business involved sales crews selling packages of roses and carnations on street corners and in busy marketplaces throughout the city. Because this part of my business was all cash and the other wholesale, I didn't give any thought to charging or collecting sales tax. During that time, I was reading the Word day and night and told the Lord that whatever I saw in His Word, I would yield myself to and draw on His grace to obey. One day, I came upon the following verse of Scripture:

> *Therefore submit yourselves to every ordinance of man for the Lord's sake.*
>
> 1 Peter 2:13

While reading this, the Holy Spirit dealt with me over the street-corner and marketplace sales portion of my business. He convicted me that it was actually retail, not wholesale, as I had convinced myself by calling my business a wholesale floral company. I needed to charge sales tax. I could not get around that truth whether the city and state ever found out about it or not.

So, I called my managers in and let them know we would be collecting and paying sales tax on this portion of the business immediately. They murmured and complained about the hassle of this new process, calling it "Greg's conscience money." But I called it the-fear-of-the-Lord money. It was just another lesson learned in following God, His Word, and His ways rather than yielding to the fear of man and opinions of my managers. This proved to be wisdom for us, resulting in a business increase of more than three times the amount of sales tax we paid. I used those numbers to teach my managers and staff that it is always right to do the right thing.

Another huge step my wife and I took in our journey of walking in the fear of the Lord had to do with following the call of God to train for full-time ministry. Earlier in life, I discovered that my obsession with success was due, in part, to my desire for approval from my dad. Now that I had built a very successful business that impressed my dad and had gained his approval, I had to decide if I was willing to give that up to follow God's call to attend Bible college. Because Janice and I had laid a foundation in the fear of the Lord and were growing in our trust of Him, this move was not as difficult as some of our earlier decisions. We were becoming less and less dependent upon the approval of man, including the approval of our parents. We ultimately left our business behind to follow God's call on our lives, bringing us increased wisdom and peace.

Though I have a lot of stories illustrating this point, Jesus is our ultimate example of walking in the fear of the Lord. The Bible reveals the many times He chose to follow His Father over the objections of His family, disciples, or the religious leaders of that day. The following passages are just a few of these examples.

> *His brothers therefore said to Him, "Depart from here and go into Judea, that Your disciples also may see the works that You are doing. For no one does anything in secret while he himself seeks to be known openly. If You do these things, show Yourself to the world." For even His brothers did not believe*

in Him. Then Jesus said to them, "My time has not yet come, but your time is always ready."

John 7:3-6

Jesus said to them [Pharisees], *"If God were your Father, you would love Me, for I proceeded forth and came from God; nor have I come of Myself, but He sent Me. Why do you not understand My speech? Because you are not able to listen to My word. You are of your father the devil…"*

John 8:42-44

As you can see by these passages of Scripture, Jesus was not trying to win a popularity contest with either His family or the Pharisees. In fact, Isaiah 11:3 tells us Jesus delighted in the fear of the Lord. He was completely committed to following His Father: only saying what He heard the Father say and only doing what He saw the Father do. Even when His close friends and disciples pleaded with Him, Jesus refused to be moved by their emotions. He followed His Father's leading.

Now Jesus loved Martha and her sister and Lazarus. So, when He heard that he [Lazarus] *was sick, He stayed two more days in the place where He was.*

John 11:5-6

The emotional pressure of others did not move Jesus in what He did and the timing of the various ministry assignments presented to Him. In this instance, Jesus waited two days before going to see Mary and Martha. By the time He got to their house, Lazarus was no longer sick; he was dead. Though Jesus subsequently raised

Lazarus from the dead, He was not moved by the fear of man—even the opinions and will of those close to Him whom He loved. Jesus was only moved by the fear of the Lord.

In my walk with God, I have learned over four decades that becoming a disciple of Jesus requires us to value the fear of the Lord over the opinions and favor of man. Jesus modeled this and it has become a passion of mine. I want to walk, and even delight, in the same measure of the fear of the Lord as He did. But there are times I find myself subtly slipping back into the fear of man.

"To fear God is to fear nothing else."

Once, during my pastorate in North Texas, Paul Milligan, an elder in my church, and I were ministering to a lady who had been part of our church in Houston, Texas. She was being oppressed by the enemy and having serious demonic attacks. They assaulted her mind and caused her to react out of control. While speaking to this woman during one of her lucid moments, Paul said something to her I will never forget. He said, "To fear God is to fear nothing else."

Wow! What a powerful statement. I don't know if this lady understood what Paul said and experienced freedom, but I know I did. In that moment, I saw that I had been afraid of everything. I had unconsciously been preparing messages to impress people, hoping they would stay in our church. I had avoided speaking on topics I thought might offend people or be controversial. I realized, through Paul's statement to this woman, that I had been yielding to the fear of man—big time! I just had not realized it.

I didn't hear another word Paul spoke to this lady. I was too busy repenting for submitting to the fear of man instead of

> I determined from that moment forward, I was going to speak the truth and stand by the truth no matter who it connected me with or separated me from.

walking in the fear of the Lord. I determined from that moment forward, I was going to speak the truth and stand by the truth no matter who it connected me with or separated me from. People's response to the Word was not my responsibility. My responsibility was to simply speak the word God put on my heart and led me to share. I was a free man that day. It was like my new-birth experience all over again. The sky was bluer, the grass greener, and the confidence, anointing, and fruitfulness of my ministry grew immensely. I didn't immediately tell Paul or our church family what had happened that day, but several people told me they could see a difference in me, my leadership, and my ministry.

In the fear of the lord there is strong confidence.
Proverbs 14:26

The fear of the Lord is a powerful spiritual principle that will set you free from the opinions and thoughts of others. It will cause you to walk in confidence in your relationship with God and your ministry to others. And it will access the mind of Christ, causing you to make good decisions—decisions that are unbiased and not influenced by people with a personal agenda. The fear of the Lord is the beginning of wisdom (Prov. 9:10). It is the way Jesus lived and the only way you and I should live. To fear God is to fear nothing else. I encourage you to join me on this amazing journey of freedom, confidence, fruitfulness, and wisdom.

Chapter 6

Follow Love

Have you ever wondered how Jesus knew the right thing to say and do in each situation He faced? How did He know what wisdom would say to the woman at the well or the woman caught in adultery (John 4 and 8:1-11)? How did He know what to tell the rich, young ruler to address the real stronghold in his life—the love of money (Mark 10:17-22)? How did He know how to answer the Pharisees when they asked by what authority He did miracles (Matt. 21:23-27)?

I don't know about you, but I have stuck my foot in my mouth and said the wrong things more times than I can count! But we cannot allow those mistakes to define us. You and I have the wisdom of God. We have the mind of Christ within us. If we will only take the time to draw that wisdom out, we too will find ourselves saying and doing what blesses, serves, and helps people. In this chapter, I want to share a principle with you that has helped me draw on God's wisdom over and over again. Some of the toughest decisions of my life have proven this principle to be true and trustworthy. And every time I have taken the time to apply this important key to my decision making, the Lord has manifested His wisdom through me. I know He will do the same for you. Let's look at some verses of Scripture that give us the foundation for this principle.

> *He who does not love does not know God, for God is love.*
>
> 1 John 4:8

> *Pursue love.*
>
> 1 Corinthians 14:1

> *Christ the power of God and the wisdom of God.*
>
> 1 Corinthians 1:24

When we connect these verses, we see that God is love, we are to pursue love, and Christ—who is love—is also the wisdom of God. In other words, as we pursue love, we will find wisdom. Following love is the key to consistently making good decisions in life. Love and wisdom are like sisters; they are connected. If you discover love, you will find wisdom. And when you find wisdom, it is because love has led you there.

As we pursue love, we will find wisdom.

One of the best examples of this principle I've found is in First Kings chapter 3. This chapter tells the story of two women with newborn sons living in the same house. One of their children died in the night. That mother switched her dead son with the living infant while the other mother was asleep. The next morning, she claimed the living infant as her own. When the other mother woke and examined the dead child lying beside her, she discovered it was not hers. Both women went before King Solomon, claiming the living child as their own. The following verses tell the rest of the story.

> Then the king said, "Bring me a sword." So they brought a sword before the king. And the king said, "Divide the living child in two, and give half to one, and half to the other." Then the woman whose son was living spoke to the king, for she yearned with compassion for her son; and she said, "O my lord, give her the living child, and by no means kill him!" But the other said, "Let him be neither mine nor yours, but divide him." So the king answered and said, "Give the first woman the living child, and by no means kill him, she is his mother." And all Israel heard of the judgment which the king had rendered; and they feared the king, for they saw that the wisdom of God was in him to administer justice.
>
> 1 Kings 3:24-28

According to First Kings, Solomon surpassed all the kings of the earth in riches and wisdom (1 Kin. 10:23). Though he told his guards to cut the child in half, he did not really intend to kill the child. As the wisest man in all the earth, Solomon used this test of love to determine the identity of the child's true mother. He knew that if he could reveal the one who truly loved the child, wisdom would also be revealed. Solomon (wisdom) knew the real mother would give up her right to the child for the life of her child. Love always gives up its own rights to ensure life.

Applying this principle of love will work for us today. If we will take the time to find out what love would do in a situation, wisdom will be there. Of course, it helps to reflect on First Corinthians 13:4-8 when considering such a decision. This passage of Scripture provides us with God's definition of love.

> *Love suffers long and is kind; love does not envy; love does not parade itself, is not puffed up; does not behave rudely, does not seek its own, is not provoked, thinks no evil; does not rejoice in iniquity, but rejoices in the truth; bears all things, believes all things, hopes all things, endures all things. Love never fails.*
>
> 1 Corinthians 13:4-8

I have also found something very practical that helps me apply this principle to my life and find God's wisdom when making an important decision. Anytime I am seeking God's wisdom for a decision regarding a situation in life, I intentionally set aside what benefits me or is the most comfortable, convenient, or expedient (the easiest path) for me. I call this "circumcising my heart" from selfish and fleshly motives. When I consciously take the time to set those options aside and consider what is best for those involved, I discover God's wisdom. This has worked again and again in my personal life as well as in business and ministry. I have faced several challenging decisions in my life and ministry that I have not felt trained or qualified to navigate. But applying this principle has helped me walk in wisdom and make good decisions on a consistent basis. Over the years, I have discovered that most difficult decisions are not a choice between good and evil but between good and best. That's why it's so important to rely on God's wisdom as it is revealed through love.

Many times, the greatest challenge in decision making is determining whether mercy or tough love is best. Each option can be love, but which is best for the person and situation you are presently dealing with? The following verses in Galatians chapter 6 reveal the importance of this distinction.

> *Bear one another's burdens, and so fulfill the law of Christ.*
>
> Galatians 6:2

> *For each one shall bear his own load.*
>
> Galatians 6:5

Each of these verses describes a different dimension of love. One is mercy—bearing another's burdens. The other is tough love—each bearing their own load. Which one is correct? Each of them has its place. Which should we apply to the decision we're presently considering? In order to determine that, we must set aside that which is easiest and most comfortable. We must choose not to consider what is convenient or beneficial for us and instead ask, "What is best for the person or group of people I'm dealing with in this situation?" Every time I have done that, I have discovered God's wisdom. That does not mean that each time I make a decision everyone agrees with me or is happy with the decision, but that decision has proven to be what is best for the ones I am serving. And I am happy knowing that I have pleased the Lord by putting others' interests ahead of my own.

Let nothing be done through selfish ambition or conceit, but in lowliness of mind let each esteem others better than himself. Let each of you look out not only for his own interests, but also for the interests of others.

Philippians 2:3-4

This is how Jesus made tough decisions. It's how He knew what to say and do in challenging and pressure-filled situations. He acted on the principle of love and walked in the fear of the Lord. He chose to make pleasing God the highest priority in His decision making. He set aside His own interests, including anything that would make Him look good, and considered what was best for the people He served.

One example of this was in the case of the woman caught in adultery in John chapter 8. The scribes and Pharisees brought this woman to Jesus while He was teaching in the temple. My first question about this situation is, where was the man? Why didn't they bring her companion in sin to Jesus? It takes two to commit adultery, you know. Most likely, the man was one of their friends or family members—or maybe even one of them, a fellow Pharisee. In any case, they told Jesus (as if He didn't know) the penalty for adultery from the law. They asked if they should stone the woman to death. They really didn't care about this woman, but they did want to find fault with Jesus. They wanted to trick Him into breaking the law. If they could accomplish that, they would have something by which to accuse and potentially get rid of Jesus. Perhaps they even planned this out, collaborating with one of their friends to seduce a woman into an adulterous relationship.

If that was the case, I'm sure they agreed to let this man go and only bring the woman before Jesus.

Whether this is what happened or not, their actions were evil to the core. They were attempting to use the law to pressure Jesus and put Him in a corner. How did Jesus respond? He ignored them. He knelt down and began writing on the ground with His finger as though He did not even hear them. I wonder what He was writing on the ground. The Bible doesn't say, but I like to think He was writing the names of the Pharisees' girlfriends. Though we don't know specifically what Jesus wrote, I'm certain that while He drew on the ground, He was taking the time to draw on His Father for wisdom. I am sure He was praying about the best course of action for this woman, the Pharisees, and others who would later hear of this situation. I'm sure He wanted to communicate God's heart for each of them and do it in a way that would not violate the law. Jesus was faced with a dilemma between the justice and judgment required of the law and mercy.

Finally, Jesus stood and said, *"He who is without sin among you, let him throw a stone at her first"* (John 8:7). He put the judgment of the law back on them, implying that their sins were as worthy of death as hers. Each of them left, from the oldest to the youngest, until only one remained—the One who was without sin—Jesus. He did not condone the woman's sin. He told her to *"go and sin no more,"* but He also showed her mercy. When none were left to condemn her, Jesus said, *"Neither do I condemn you"* (John 8:1-11).

What a powerful example of how Jesus took time to draw on the Father's wisdom and seek Him about what was best for all in this situation. Jesus found the wisdom of God by following the way of love. He did not violate the law but allowed mercy to triumph over judgment (James 2:13)! That is how Jesus accessed wisdom, and that is how you and I can access wisdom—even in the most challenging and pressure-filled situations.

Wisdom in Family Decisions

My wife and I have three sons and one daughter. Several years ago, about six months apart, two of my three sons called late at night—from jail. I won't reveal which of them called me, and please don't ask. I have no wish to uncover their sin or cause them condemnation but only want to use their stories as an example for you. Today, each of my sons is following the Lord. They are amazing men of God, great husbands and fathers, and I am very proud of them. But they do not have mistake-free lives, as I am sure none of us can claim, either. In the first case, my son called from jail at about 12:30 in the morning.

As soon as I answered the phone, he said, "Dad, come pick me up from jail." I asked what he had done to be put in jail, and he said, "I ran a stop sign. A police car tried to pull me over, and I tried to outrun the police. They caught me and put me in jail. Come get me, Dad."

To give you some background, at this time, our son had made a habit of violating the boundaries we had set for him. He was breaking curfew and being dishonest about where he was going and who he was with. He was in a season of rebellion, and none of the consequences he had received had been adequate in turning his heart around. Though I only had a minute or two to decide how to respond in this situation, before answering him, I told his mom what was going on and prayed.

As I was praying quietly to myself, I heard, "Tell him you will see him in the morning." I knew from this word that the best thing for my son at this time was some "tough love" from Dad. So, that is what I told him. He didn't like it, but he also never forgot that night. And he hasn't attempted to outrun the police since!

About six months later, another of our sons called me around midnight. He said, "Dad, I'm in jail. Can you come get me?" I asked him what he had done to be put in jail, and he said, "I had a blowout on one of my tires, and a policeman pulled over to assist me. While he was there, he checked my license and found an unpaid ticket in my file from six months ago. I got pulled over in a small town several miles away, but I lost the ticket, Dad. I forgot the name of the town, so I didn't take care of it. I'm sorry to bother you and Mom so late, but I'll pay you back whatever it costs."

This situation was altogether different. I could hear the humility in my son's voice. He was willing to take responsibility for his actions and did not make excuses. I leaned over and told his mom what he said and spent a moment in prayer. This time, I heard, "Go pick him up, take him to Denny's, and don't say a word about his mistake." So, that is what I did. He also remembers that instance to this day.

Each of these instances showed our boys love. Though it wasn't easy for me to let one of my sons spend the night in jail, it was wisdom—the tough love he needed—in that situation. It also wasn't easy for me to do something entirely different for my other son. I didn't want it to look like I was favoring one over the other. But he needed mercy. It was what was best for him in that situation. I had to learn to trust God with each of my boys and look to wisdom for my response. The bottom line is, ask the Holy Spirit to show you which principle of the Word is in the best interest of those you are serving. Decisions are easy when faced with the choice between good and evil. But decisions become more difficult when there is more than one principle from the Word that could apply to the situation in front of you, and those principles seem to oppose each other. In those cases, take the time to set aside the options that benefit you and consider which option will benefit those you are serving. God will make the best choice clear.

Give where you have joy; don't give where you don't have joy. And don't allow yourself to be condemned about not giving where you don't have joy.

Joy-Directed Giving

One thing that has helped me sort out which of these aspects of love I should act on is understanding the principle revealed in the following verse of Scripture.

So let each one give as he purposes in his heart, not grudgingly or of necessity; for God loves a cheerful giver.

2 Corinthians 9:7

I used to read this verse in a legalistic mindset, as if God were saying, "Boy, you better be cheerful when you give." But that is not what He is telling us here. God revealed His heart behind this verse to me by saying that cheerfulness—or joy—should be the barometer for our giving. Give where you have joy; don't give where you don't have joy. And don't allow yourself to be condemned about not giving where you don't have joy.

In our personal lives, Janice and I have always given to the poor and to those in need. This has been a part of our heart and practice in ministry as well. Years ago, our church building in North Texas was located one block from a major highway. Because of our location, many homeless people and those in need stopped by our church, asking for help. We always helped feed people who were hungry and often helped people catch up on their utility bills and pay their rent. Sometimes we purchased bus tickets to help those in need get home to their families.

Once, a man new to the area needed help for a few days before he could start his new job. We bought him a nice meal and paid for a couple of nights in a motel room. The next day, I sent one of my staff members by his room to drop off lunch. We found the man had invited his girlfriend to stay with him at the motel. When he called later to ask our church to provide him with a few additional nights at the motel, we refused. When he asked for more food, I again said no. We were not going to pay for that man to violate God's Word and sleep with his girlfriend in a motel room we provided. I did not have joy facilitating his lifestyle of sin, so we stopped giving to him. Though he accused me of not being merciful and loving, I did not allow myself to be condemned over it. There were other people our church could help who would use that help the right way.

Listen, my dear brothers and sisters, the decision we made to cease helping that man was acting in love toward him! Love and truth work together. We cannot demonstrate God's love to someone by violating the truth.

> *Grace, mercy, and peace will be with you from God the Father and from the Lord Jesus Christ, the Son of the Father, in truth and love.*
>
> 2 John 1:3

> *My little children, let us not love in word or in tongue, but in deed and in truth.*
>
> 1 John 3:18

What I am sharing with you is wisdom. There are times to show mercy. There are times to show tough love. Don't allow yourself to feel condemned for showing tough love to those who need tough love. And don't let others pressure you into showing tough love to those who need mercy.

> Don't allow yourself to feel condemned for showing tough love to those who need tough love. And don't let others pressure you into showing tough love to those who need mercy.

Years ago, a woman in our church was unintentionally causing strife with other members of our church family. A couple of our leaders confronted her one-on-one about the problem, but it persisted. So, I called her into my office, with another staff member present, for the purpose of confronting and correcting her behavior and treatment of others. As I started to correct her, I instead found myself encouraging and thanking her for her faithful service in the church. My staff member looked at me in shock, but the woman broke down in tears. She confessed that she had been fearful of our meeting and felt like she was being called into the principal's office. She said she knew she had been treating people poorly and asked our forgiveness. The mercy and goodness of God was wisdom for this woman in this situation. Because I showed her mercy, it brought about repentance.

> *The goodness of God leads you to repentance.*
>
> Romans 2:4

Following love allows you to access the wisdom of God and the mind of Christ in every situation. Lay aside any consideration of what is best for you. Remember that **comfort, convenience, and expedience (that which is easiest for you) are the enemies of wisdom**. Circumcise your heart from selfish motives and focus on what is best for those you are serving, those who will be impacted by your decisions. That is how you pursue love. That is also how God's wisdom is made available to you.

Chapter 7

Seek Counsel

A s we begin this chapter focused on seeking counsel for the purpose of drawing out wisdom, it brings some obvious questions to mind: Why is it necessary to seek counsel when the Word says we already have the mind of Christ? Isn't the Word enough for us to access the mind of Christ and make good decisions? What if the counsel we receive is wrong? How do we judge the counsel we receive from others accurately? How do we know when it is appropriate to act on someone's counsel and when it is not? How can we know who to trust in receiving godly counsel?

I will address each of these questions throughout the chapter, but first, we need to understand the importance of being open to counsel from others. Each of us has our own perspective, but no matter how accurate our perspective is or how much of it comes from the Word, it is still limited. First Corinthians says we all *"know in part"* (I Cor. 13:9). You and I know what we know. But that knowledge is only *"in part."* It is partial. None of us have the whole loaf. None of us have all revelation or the last word on any subject. Some who have not spent time in or valued the Word, have an even more limited perspective. But no matter how much of the Word we know, each of our perspectives is still limited. You and I know what we know, but godly counsel exposes us to increased perspective. Consider the following scriptures as evidence of this fact:

> *With the well-advised is wisdom.*
>
> Proverbs 13:10

> *Listen to counsel and receive instruction, that you may be wise in your latter days.*
>
> Proverbs 19:20

> *For by wise counsel you will wage your own war, and in a multitude of counselors there is safety.*
>
> Proverbs 24:6

Each of these powerful verses reveals our need for godly counsel. They show us a definite connection between receiving counsel and accessing wisdom. The first listed verse (Prov. 13:10) declares that wisdom comes to us as a result of being well advised. That means we need to make ourselves available to receiving counsel. The second verse (Prov. 19:20) adds another dimension to this principle. It tells us to listen to counsel and be open to receiving instruction. If we approach counsel as if we already know what to do, we are just checking off a scriptural requirement and the counselor cannot add anything to us. We will not be wise in our latter days. That is pride. Pride fails to receive the grace of God and limits us to the wisdom and knowledge we currently possess. Will Rogers a wise, Oklahoma humorist, once said, "Everybody is ignorant, only on different subjects" That is so true. We cannot fully grow in wisdom if we do nothing to remedy our ignorance by failing to seek wise counsel.

We cannot fully grow in wisdom if we do nothing to remedy our ignorance by failing to seek wise counsel.

The third verse listed above and found in Proverbs 24:6 reveals additional benefits of receiving counsel. It tells us that waging war (or we could say, accomplishing kingdom purposes that have the potential of destroying the enemy's kingdom) requires wise counsel. It also tells us that our safety is a direct result of surrounding ourselves with a team of counselors. There is real value in receiving counsel from more than one source. It keeps us safe from major mistakes and helps us identify and cover areas of vulnerability. We need the counsel of others to help us fulfill the vision and dreams God has put in our hearts. He has not called us to fulfill His will and plan alone, but in teams. Making yourself available to godly counsel will help you fulfill His will for your life. It will also enable you to become part of helping others fulfill God's will for their lives.

How to Receive Counsel

In the late 1990s, I had the opportunity to spend one week a year for four consecutive years being mentored by Jack Hayford at the School of Pastoral Nurture. Each year, he invited thirty-five to forty pastors to spend the week with him. During that time, he imparted principles of wisdom to us that he had gleaned from God's

Word and applied in his ministry that helped him fulfill God's call on his life. It was a valuable and life-changing experience for me to hear how he measured and experienced success by kingdom, rather than worldly, standards.

During one of those weeks, Pastor Jack shared the story of how he received the second campus for their church, The Church on the Way, in Van Nuys, California. Their church had grown significantly, and they were not able to accommodate its growth in the building they owned. They were already holding multiple services each weekend but still couldn't accommodate all the people God was bringing in. One day as he was driving, he noticed a "for sale" sign on a building less than two miles from their church. As he sat waiting at a red light near the property, he heard the Holy Spirit say, "I am giving you this building. It is yours." Pastor Jack didn't immediately act on what he heard. He first prayed about it for several days and then set a meeting with his church board to discuss the opportunity.

When Pastor Jack met with his board, he did not tell them, "The Lord spoke to me and said He is giving us this building. It is ours." Instead, he told them he had noticed a church building for sale near their current facility, and after praying about it, sensed the Lord's leading to discuss the possibility of purchasing it. This was a real lesson of kingdom leadership for me. I remember him saying that even when the Lord speaks clearly to him about something related to the church, he rarely tells others that the Lord said to do this or that. Instead, he typically says "This is what I am sensing the Lord leading us to do. What are your thoughts? Do you have any input to share?"

When we go to someone for counsel and say, "The Lord told me this," we tie that person's hands. If they are a believer (and they should be a believer if we are going to them for godly counsel), the only responses we leave them with are "I agree with you" or "I don't think that is the Lord."

In this case, Jack Hayford's board checked out the building, inspecting its price and renovation needs, and came back to him, saying, "We don't think it is prudent to purchase that building at this time. They are asking too much, and it will be a costly remodel for us to bring it up to standards and move in." Initially, Pastor Jack was disappointed. But he accepted their counsel without using the "God told me" card. He simply trusted God to bring to pass what he believed God has spoken to him. He did not manipulate his board with "But God told me it was ours."

Several weeks passed, and another church put a contract on the building. In the process of their inspection, they discovered major asbestos removal was required before they could move in. Because of the high cost involved, they backed out of their sales contract, and the original owners became responsible for the asbestos removal. Once removal was complete, the building went up for sale again, this time at a lower price. When Pastor Jack and the board discovered all that had transpired, they agreed to purchase the building and were able to remodel it to meet city codes and their church standards within budget. What a testimony of the importance of valuing godly counsel and using that counsel to receive God's wisdom! Pastor Jack's submission allowed God to fulfill His word while saving the church hundreds of thousands of dollars. That is wisdom, my friends.

I have applied this principle of receiving godly counsel both as a pastor and in my leadership roles at Andrew Wommack Ministries and Charis Bible College, and I have found it to be a lifesaver time and time again. Whenever I know God has spoken to me, I go to trusted men and women I am in relationship with, to my church leaders, or to my ministry leadership team and say, "I am sensing the Lord's leading in this. Would you give me your honest feedback?" A majority of the time, the responses I get from those to whom I appeal for godly counsel do not change what God has spoken to me. But they do give me a wiser perspective on the how and when of what God said. I nearly always discover better strategies and/or consider different timings in accomplishing what God has spoken to me. I cannot remember a single time I have asked for counsel in this way that I was not better off for receiving it.

Ecclesiastes 8:6 says, "*To every purpose there is time and judgment*" (KJV). This verse identifies three primary areas where we need to discover God's wisdom when following His direction for the vision, dream, or kingdom purpose He has put in our hearts. The first area is the purpose or "what" God has asked of, directed, or assigned to you and your team. The second is timing. "When" are you to start the project, and what time frame will its fulfillment be linked to? The third area where we need to uncover God's wisdom includes the judgment, or strategy plan, for the vision. It is the "how" of accomplishing what God has initiated.

I am a visionary. Whenever I hear that God wants me and my team to do something, I am ready to jump right away. But I have learned over the years that just because I know the "what" of a project does not mean my team and I are prepared to launch that project. We also need to know the "when" and "how" for a project to be successful. Launching prematurely—without counsel, strategic planning, and preparation—can actually be the downfall of a project or cause what God has put in my heart to fail. That is not wisdom. I have learned that drawing up a strategy plan with my team that will help us fulfill what God has spoken is very valuable. Often, once the right strategic plan has been developed, I know God's timing is close.

I have learned that launching a God-ordained kingdom project prematurely is like having a spiritual miscarriage or abortion. Many premature births in the kingdom of God are stillborn because the leader failed to receive wise counsel. They do not have a strategy for what has been conceived in their hearts, and they do not know its timing. Strategy and timing almost always correspond to each other and are necessary components of the wisdom needed to fulfill God's purposes and plans for our lives. And a majority of the time, they come by valuing and heeding wise counsel.

How to Judge Counsel

Let me make something very clear: You and I are not obligated to act on all the counsel we receive, even from mature, trustworthy leaders. It is our responsibility to ensure their counsel lines up with God's written Word, our own spirits, and other trustworthy leaders in relationship with us. Correctly judging counsel is similar to judging prophetic words. According to Scripture, no prophetic word or word of counsel stands alone. We are not obligated to act on any of it without first testing and proving it.

By the mouth of two or three witnesses every word shall be established.

2 Corinthians 13:1

Test all things; hold fast what is good.

1 Thessalonians 5:21

I refuse to act on any individual's counsel or prophetic word until I have had opportunity to pray over it, spend time in the Word, and seek additional counsel from other leaders I trust. Until I can pass it through those tests, I set that word on the shelf and do not allow it to put pressure on me or condemn me while I wait on the Lord. This has proven to be wisdom to me and has kept me safe from making decisions on something I have not yet tested.

A number of years ago, I sought the counsel of a trusted minister who came to our church. He had visited several times and always had a good word that ministered life to our people. This time, I sought his counsel, asking if he saw anything in our church body that might be hindering our growth or could help us grow more. His immediate response was, "There is not a clear sound of unity in your church. There is a lack of clarity of vision and not one sound that people can rally around."

When he said that, it just did not bear witness in my heart. We had a clear vision that we communicated regularly to our people— helping people achieve their dreams, grow in Christlikeness, and change their world. Our church leadership team had never experienced a greater unity than we were at that time. And his immediate response to me without any thought or consideration was concerning. It was as if he had been thinking about my question before I asked and had already made a judgment without discussing it with me or any of our church leaders. I shared what he told me with a couple of my elders, and they immediately dismissed his counsel. They did not believe it applied to us. Because it did not bear witness in my heart or with two trusted leaders in the church, I set his words aside. This did not mean I considered him a false prophet or false teacher, but neither did I go back to him for counsel.

The following traits describe a person you and I can trust to give godly counsel:

1. **They know God** and have an intimate relationship with the Father.
2. **They know the Word.** It is risky to receive counsel from someone who gives you their experience and opinions but doesn't know the Word.
3. **They are available.** Will they make time for you?
4. **They are authentic.** They are genuine and transparent, willing to share their mistakes and failures with you, as well as their successes, as a mode of learning.
5. **They are mature.** They have developed character and integrity in their life.
6. **They encourage you.** They believe in you; they encourage and build you up.
7. **They have strength.** The person you go to for counsel needs to have some experience or skill they have developed that they will freely share with you.
8. **They have a hearing ear.** They have learned to hear God, and they listen to you.

9. **They are objective.** Their counsel is not biased with prejudice or opinion.
10. **They are patient.** They are not pushy with you but willing to wait on God and give you time to "get it."
11. **They are compassionate**, merciful, and kind, not judgmental or condemning.
12. **They are trustworthy.** They keep the things you share in confidence.

Not every person you or I go to for counsel will have all of these traits, but they should demonstrate many of them to be counted as a person we can trust to give us good, godly, consistent counsel. Pastor Bob Nichols is one of my most trusted counselors. I have gone to him several times when dealing with a crisis and am in need of wisdom. He has been faithful to listen to my situations thoroughly, pray over them, and then give me good counsel that has consistently proven itself to be wisdom from God for me, my church, and my ministry.

The first time I went to him for counsel, Janice and I were going through a frivolous, nine-million-dollar lawsuit and involuntary church plant (church split). Pastor Bob spent time with me, gave me counsel on what he would do in my situation, and gave me his card and personal phone number. He said if, after we acted on his counsel, everything "hit the fan," to give him a call. Everything more than "hit the fan" after that, so I called him. He made himself available for us and came to mediate a very difficult meeting.

At this time, several elders who had left our church were fighting with the new elders over our church building. Pastor

Bob came that night, and God used him powerfully to bring peace between the two groups and an end to the dispute over the building. He also helped us determine who should lead the church going forward. Pastor Bob then wrote a letter I was able to read to the entire church body that God used to bring peace to our church family. God saved our church through our relationship with Pastor Bob Nichols, and it all began with one meeting to receive counsel.

"Whatever success I have achieved in life and ministry is due to these two principles: I stay childlike with God and teachable with men."

I have discovered that major kingdom relationships and connections are established through times of counsel. Wise counsel is essential when the time frame for a decision is limited. That counsel will keep you safe and keep you from making emotional decisions. Receiving counsel that will bring wisdom requires humility on your part. Pride does not receive the benefit of counsel or the wisdom that comes from it.

> *When pride comes, then comes shame; but with the humble is wisdom.*
>
> Proverbs 11:2

Something Jack Hayford said to our group of pastors during one of our weeks together has proven to be wisdom in my life. He said, "Whatever success I have achieved in life and ministry is due to these two principles: I stay childlike with God and teachable with men." This wisdom has helped me to stay open to counsel and, in turn, helped me access God's wisdom in my life. I am convinced it will do the same for you.

Chapter 8

Be Selective of Your Close Relationships

We've shared how wisdom can come to us through godly counsel. In this chapter, I want to talk about the next level of relationships when it comes to receiving wisdom through others. It is true that wisdom can come to us by way of counsel, yet an even greater measure of wisdom—or lack of it—can come through our close, inner circle of relationships. Let's look at the following verses in the Word of God that confirm this truth.

> *He who walks with wise men will be wise, but the companion of fools will be destroyed.*
>
> Proverbs 13:20

The righteous should choose his friends carefully,
for the way of the wicked leads them astray.

Proverbs 12:26

Show me your
friends and I
will show you
your future.

We cannot afford to gloss over these truths. Those people we choose as our closest friends, our inner circle, will influence our potential in life. Show me your friends and I will show you your future. My good friend Billy Epperhart once said, "You cannot fly with the eagles hanging out with the turkeys." Flying with eagles requires making eagles part of your inner circle of relationships.

The friends we choose tells us a lot about how we feel about ourselves. The verse I referenced in Proverbs chapter 12 instructs us to choose our friends carefully. That means we need to be selective and intentional about our close relationships. We can love everyone and treat all people with kindness and respect, but we must be selective about those we allow into our inner circle. Remember that Jesus, our example, prayed all night before selecting the disciples He would allow into His inner circle. I encourage you to be equally prayerful and thoughtful about who you allow into your closest circle of friends.

Be careful about becoming close friends with people who consistently whine, murmur, complain, blame-shift, speak negatively of those in authority, and talk about other friends behind their backs. These are not character traits of those you want in your inner circle. If one of your "friends" is talking about others behind their backs, you must realize it won't be long before they are talking about you behind your back.

If you are struggling with a low self-image, you will be tempted to hang out with those who are also part of the "wounded hearts club." This group of friends finds solace by comforting each other over things done wrong to them. Their common bond is having mutual enemies. These types of relationships lead to blame-shifting societies and "victims anonymous" clubs. This circle of broken, wounded hearts pass out gold membership cards to anyone who will help them maintain their victimhood and make an enemy of those who have hurt or disenfranchised them in some way. They develop entitlement attitudes and judgments against others, especially those in authority. There is no wisdom in such relationships!

When it comes to others, expect nothing and be thankful for everything.

Jesus said that life would not be offense free. *"Then He said to the disciples, 'It is impossible that no offenses should come'"* (Luke 17:1). It is not possible to go through life and have no offenses come your way. Offense will come to each of us, and many times, it comes through our closest relationships. The reason we are so vulnerable to offense is that we have too many expectations on those in our closest circle of relationships. But I have learned something that has helped me stay free from offense in relationship: When it comes to others, expect nothing and be thankful for everything. There is freedom in that. If I am not expecting something, I cannot be offended by someone.

If someone in my inner circle does disappoint me in some way, I choose to let love cover it and give them mercy, just as I would like to receive mercy (1 Pet. 4:8 and Matt. 5:7). If any of your close friends are easily offended, it will eventually impact you.

If someone in your inner circle is funny and fun to hang out with but has habits of lying, cheating, stealing, and speaking negatively about others, don't be deceived. That too will influence you if you don't address it.

> *Do not be deceived: "Evil company corrupts good habits* [morals].*"*
>
> 1 Corinthians 15:33

My wife and I pastored two churches in Texas over twenty-seven years. The last church we served in as pastors was in North Texas. We were there for twenty-four years. Over that period of time, we observed this principle confirmed in multitudes of teenagers and adults.

Two teenage girls I will call Amy and Dee Ann, each came from good families where their parents lived and modeled the Word of God. They established the right balance of love and discipline in their homes. Our youth pastor came to us at different times to tell us that Amy and Dee Ann were hanging out with the wrong group of teenagers. Though we had a good-size youth group, each girl avoided becoming close friends with the strong, mature leaders of the group. Rather, they chose to be close with the immature, hurting, and troubled youth. I instructed our youth pastor to reach out to Amy's and Dee Ann's parents and encourage them to get involved with their daughters' choice of close friends.

In each case, Amy and Dee Ann refused to listen to their parents and youth pastor and persisted in maintaining their troubled relationships. After graduating high school and the youth group, I monitored their progress from time to time through my relationship with their parents. Sadly, each of them struggled with broken relationships, divorce, and other problems for many years. I am glad to report that both girls seem to be doing better today, but all of the pain, struggle, and trouble they experienced could have been avoided by choosing better friends. That pain was not God's best for them and certainly not His wisdom.

The Word of God is true. Bad friendships corrupt good morals (1 Cor. 15:33). But walking with wise men and women will make us wiser (Prov. 13:20). Before I move on to focus on the positive aspects of choosing good relationships, I want to help those who have realized their inner circle of friends is not best for them. I am not suggesting you completely cut off relationship with those who are in this category, though you may have to do that with some. I recommend easing your way out of those relationships by finding other healthy friendships. Spend more time with healthy friends and get involved with a good local church. Become part of that church's small groups and make yourself available to others your age. Be willing to deal with rejection initially, as not everyone will respond to your effort to make new friends, but keep trying. I believe God has divine connections, divine appointments, and open doors in relationship for you. He will bring those into your life as you commit to walk with wise men and women rather than stumble around with the foolish and ungodly.

Each of us needs relationships that are emotionally healthy and centered around Jesus. Any relationship that consistently drains your emotional tank or attempts to keep your focus on self is unhealthy. That should be a warning sign to you. If you have such a relationship, begin to move away from it or cut it off altogether. I am constantly looking for "God connections" in relationships. I want relationships where we have a mutual love and appreciation for each other and are encouraging (and sometimes challenging) each other to take our places and fulfill God's plans for our lives.

Pastor Bob and Joy Nichols have been this kind of relationship for Janice and me. Throughout our lives and ministry, they have always encouraged us to keep our focus on Jesus. They challenge us to live lives of faith and trust in Jesus no matter what we are going through. Our relationship with our pastors has been a constant source of strength and has helped us stay the course when fighting battles of discouragement or when we felt like quitting.

> *As iron sharpens iron, so a man sharpens the countenance of his friend.*
>
> Proverbs 27:17

Even in the world, we can see this principle of iron sharpening iron and walking with the wise bringing wisdom to us through our relationships. Bill Belichick, one of the most successful coaches in NFL history, was tutored by Bill Parcells, a Super Bowl–winning coach with the New York Giants. Roy Williams, a very successful college basketball coach at both the University of Kansas and the University of North Carolina, was once an assistant for Dean Smith, a successful coach with the University of North Carolina who won two national championships and appeared in eleven Final Four games. We can see this same pattern with CEOs. Many corporations develop new leaders under those who have already become successful CEOs. Jack Welch, the former CEO of General Electric, developed a training program for leaders in his company that produced several successful businessmen and women.

In the kingdom of God, this principle operates the same way. I have observed a number of ministry leaders, such as Kenneth Hagin, Kenneth Copeland, and Andrew Wommack, who have raised up thousands of other ministers through their ministries. Many pastors have done the same. There are scores of pastors I know personally who have built successful churches by starting out under Pastor John Osteen's, Pastor Bob Nichols', and Pastor Jack Hayford's ministries. My good friend Wendell Parr has shared with me how much John Osteen and Bob Nichols influenced his pastorate in North Texas and his teaching ministry today.

When selecting friends to be part of your inner circle you want to make sure they are people who will sharpen you, challenge you, and encourage you in your walk with the Lord.

A good measure of my ministry success is due to my relationship with other ministries where I have served or studied under and observed, including Pastor John Osteen, Kenneth Hagin, Jack Hayford, Andrew Wommack, and Pastor Bob Nichols. I learned different leadership principles from each of these powerful men of God, and each was influential in imparting God's wisdom to me—wisdom I would not have received without my relationship with them. I once told Bob Nichols, "I want to be like you when I grow up."

Different Levels of Relationships

When selecting friends to be part of your inner circle, you want to make sure they are people who will sharpen you, challenge you, and encourage you in your walk with the Lord. If you want to grow in wisdom and walk in success, look around you and identify some men and women you respect who have experienced a measure of success, favor, and wisdom in their lives.

There are three levels of relationship each of us need to be sharpened with wisdom, character, vision, and faith. We all need:

1. **Mentors/spiritual fathers** – those we look up to for counsel and who are models of wisdom, character, and success for us.
2. **Peers** – those who encourage us, challenge us, and hold us accountable to the Word and God's call on our lives.
3. **Disciples** – those we are pouring into and modeling the Word for.

We cannot force any level of these relationships, but we do need to be aware of them and make ourselves available to having all three types in our lives. Without all three, there is a danger of becoming imbalanced in our relationships. If all you have are mentoring relationships, you can become dependent on them instead of depending on God. If all you have are peer relationships, you can develop a backslapping, feel-good club where there is no real accountability. If all you have are discipling relationships, you can end up ministering out of a need to be needed and develop a "savior mentality" with those you are discipling.

Let me encourage you to make yourself available to build relationships with people who have traveled further down the roads of wisdom, character, and success than you. Serve them.

Invest in them. Observe their lives and listen to their counsel. A wisdom statement I once received from Pastor Bob Nichols is, "Sow where you want to go." In other words, find someone who is successful and bearing fruit in an area God has called you to go, and invest in them. For example, if you want a successful marriage, spend time with couples who have experienced success in their marriages. Find areas where you can serve them, listen to them, and observe their lives. God's wisdom for your successful marriage will come as a result of your relationship with them.

If you want to run a successful business, intern with a successful business owner. Apply for an entry-level position with the goal of learning the principles, systems, and culture of that business. At a minimum, invite a successful business owner to dinner and pick their brain, listening for the key principles they attribute their success to. Just make sure you pick up the tab! Billionaire Warren Buffet said, "Much of what you become in life depends on whom you choose to admire and copy."

Servanthood is one of the primary places of promotion.

Another wisdom quote from Pastor Bob is, "What you make happen for others, God will make happen for you." What are you passionate about? What do you feel called to do in life? Pray and find someone who has been doing what you want better and longer than you. Go serve them. Sow into them; observe how they are fulfilling the call of God on their lives, and as much as possible, build relationship with them. Invest your time and finances in them. Listen to their counsel, and wisdom will be released to you! If you want to go into ministry, for example, find a successful ministry that is close to what you feel called to do and volunteer to serve where they need you. Become a Joshua to a Moses. Become an Elisha to an Elijah in that ministry. Servanthood is one of the primary places of promotion. But it also positions you to see behind the scenes as to how a ministry's infrastructure plays into their success. It shows you how a successful ministry deals with people and selects key staff members. In some cases, you will learn what to avoid, but in others, you will learn how the fulfillment of God's plans and purposes relies on appropriate team strategy and timing. In both cases, that is wisdom.

Who are your close friends? Who are the role models you have chosen for your life? Those relationships will shape your future and impart wisdom to you.

Chapter 9

Stay Filled with the Spirit

Have you ever known someone so full of the Spirit that it draws you to Jesus? I am not talking about a person who is so heavenly minded they are no earthly good. Those folks act super spiritual, but they are just religious and condescending. No, I am talking about those people who truly manifest Jesus. They model Jesus and make you want to know and be like Jesus too. There is an obvious character distinction between believers who are full of the Spirit and those who are born again but still carnal.

Carnal Christians focus on the things of this world. They are led by their emotions. Their peace and happiness are controlled by the circumstances surrounding them. On the other hand, believers who are filled with the Spirit are infectious with love, joy, peace, and a positive outlook on life. They are yielded to and led by the Spirit rather than by their emotions. In life, these people model a life of trusting in the Lord rather than leaning to their own understanding (Prov. 3:5-6). Believers who are full of the Spirit are motivated by the joy of the Lord and always seem to experience a peace that surpasses their understanding (Phil. 4:7). These are the people of faith I am drawn to. These are the people I want to grow with and learn from, the people that I want to be around.

Being filled with the Spirit is important to our walk with Christ and our development of wisdom. It is one of the character traits the Lord looks for when selecting and promoting leaders in His kingdom. In Acts chapter 6, the apostles needed to delegate some of their administrative duties to other leaders within the church so that they could focus on prayer and the ministry of the Word. The following verse reveals what character traits the apostles looked for in those they would entrust to delegate this responsibility.

> *Therefore, brethren, seek out from among you seven men of good reputation, full of the Holy Spirit and wisdom, whom we may appoint over this business.*
>
> Acts 6:3

Notice the three primary traits mentioned in this passage. These traits are essential for kingdom leadership: being of good reputation, full of the Holy Spirit, and full of wisdom. But how were these traits seen? Good works and good fruit must have been manifest in each of these men's lives or others would not have been able to attest to their good reputations. Good results tied to these seven men's decision making must have also been obvious to reveal that they walked in the wisdom of God. So, if it was possible for others to observe and attest to the fact that these men were of good reputation and full of wisdom, it must have also been possible for others to observe in a tangible way that each was full of the Holy Spirit. And if it was possible then, it is also possible now. You and I should be able to distinguish between believers who are full of the Holy Spirit and those who are not. And like the apostles, we should use that information when considering who to promote to leadership roles.

I also want you to notice the strong connection between each of these godly leadership traits. A good leader will possess each trait. You cannot isolate any one trait from another and become a leader God and others will trust. In light of the subject matter of this book, *Walking in Wisdom*, I also want to point out the connection between being full of the Spirit and full of wisdom.

What It Means to Be Filled with the Spirit

I have been involved in several passionate discussions over the years regarding the different viewpoints of what it means to be filled with the Spirit. I have chosen not to debate with others over this, and I remain open to what anyone points out to me in the Word regarding this subject. But I cannot say the same is true of some with whom I've spoken. Over the years, I have found many Christians are unteachable when it comes to this topic of being filled with the Spirit. Their minds are made up. It seems they have made up their minds about other topics too, especially the gifts of the Spirit and healing. They are like concrete: thoroughly mixed and well set. And while I refuse to judge those in such a condition, I pray that the eyes of their understanding be opened to the truth (Eph. 1:17-19). I know I don't have the last word on this or any subject in the Bible. That keeps me teachable and open to more truth. God has shown me, through my study of His Word and receiving sound teaching from other trusted ministers, there are some truths you can count on regarding what it means to be filled with the Spirit.

Walking in wisdom is a fruit of staying full of the Spirit.

As we move through this chapter, you will see that walking in wisdom is a fruit of staying full of the Spirit. But notice what Jesus said in John 20 about the Holy Spirit. This is the first truth I want to bring to your attention. According to Jesus' words here, each of us receives a measure of the Spirit at the new birth.

So Jesus said to them again, "Peace to you! As the Father has sent Me, I also send you." And when He had said this, He breathed on them, and said to them, "Receive the Holy Spirit."

John 20:21-22

I believe this pre-Pentecost account is when Jesus' disciples were born again. By this time, Jesus had died on the cross for all sin and had risen from the dead. Prior to this, each of Jesus' disciples had confessed Him as Lord and they now believed that He had risen from the dead. According to Romans 10:9-10, they were saved. Jesus then breathed on them and imparted the Holy Spirit to each of them. They received a measure of the Holy Spirit at the new birth. Jesus describes this aspect of receiving the Spirit in John 4.

But whosoever drinketh of the water that I shall give him shall never thirst; but the water that I shall give him shall be in him a well of water springing up into everlasting life.

John 4:14 KJV

Notice Jesus describes this aspect of receiving the Spirit as a well of everlasting life, referencing the work of the Spirit within us at the new birth when we receive Jesus as Lord of our life. We can see from these two verses of Scripture that Jesus' disciples had been born again and received a measure of the Holy Spirit at the new birth, yet Jesus goes on to tell them to wait in Jerusalem until they received the promised outpouring of the Holy Spirit.

> *Behold, I send the Promise of My Father upon you; but tarry in the city of Jerusalem until you are endued with power from on high.*
>
> Luke 24:49

After Jesus' ascension, the disciples went to Jerusalem and waited together for the outpouring of the Spirit He had promised. And when the Day of Pentecost arrived, they were all *filled* with the Holy Spirit.

> *When the Day of Pentecost had fully come, they were all with one accord in one place. And suddenly there came a sound from heaven, as of a rushing mighty wind, and it filled the whole house where they were sitting. ... And they were all filled with the Holy Spirit and began to speak with other tongues, as the Spirit gave them utterance.*
>
> Acts 2:1-2, 4

If the disciples received the Holy Spirit at the new birth as the Scripture reveals and that was all of the Spirit they needed, why would Jesus tell them to wait for another outpouring of the Spirit? The disciples received the Spirit at the new birth when

Jesus breathed on them (John 20:21-22). But that experience was not equivalent to the promised infilling of the Spirit fulfilled in Acts chapter 2.

I want to submit to you that receiving the Spirit at the new birth and being filled with the Spirit (as the disciples were at Pentecost) are two separate experiences. And the disciples needed both. It is possible for an individual to receive the Lord and never be filled with the Spirit or receive the evidence of that filling, a spiritual prayer language often referred to as tongues. Jesus references this experience in John chapter 7.

> *On the last day, that great day of the feast, Jesus stood and cried out, saying, "If anyone thirsts, let him come to Me and drink. He who believes in Me, as the Scripture has said, out of his heart will flow rivers of living water." But this He spoke concerning the Spirit, whom those believing in Him would receive.*
>
> John 7:37-39

In John chapter 4, Jesus spoke of one work of the Spirit in the new birth. He compared that to a well of water in us when we receive Him as Lord. Here, in John chapter 7, Jesus speaks of another work of the Spirit, one in which we are filled to overflowing. Jesus compares this baptism of the Spirit to rivers of living water flowing out of us. These are two separate experiences available to every believer.

> *Then Peter said to them, "Repent, and let every one of you be baptized in the name of Jesus Christ*

for the remission of sins; and you shall receive the gift of the Holy Spirit. For the promise is to you and to your children, and to all who are afar off, as many as the Lord our God will call."

Acts 2:38-39

Have you been born again and become a child of God? Then this promise of the Spirit is for you. For this promise—as all God's promises—does not expire. The gift of the Holy Spirit is available to you today if you will simply ask for it. Jesus encouraged every born-again child of God to ask the Father for this gift of being filled with the Holy Spirit.

If you then, being evil [or human], *know how to give good gifts to your children, how much more will your heavenly Father give the Holy Spirit to those who ask Him!*

Luke 11:13

The context of this verse is a child asking their father for food—a good gift that would nourish and bless them, a gift every child should expect their father to supply. Jesus then instructed the children of God—those already saved—to ask their heavenly Father for the Holy Spirit in the same way and with the same expectation of good. If we received all of the Spirit we needed at the new birth, why, my friends, would Jesus instruct us to ask the Father for what we already have? The answer is simple: because there is more of the Holy Spirit for you and me to receive.

You can receive this gift right now. Simply pray this prayer with me:

Father, I thank You that when I received Jesus as my Lord, I received the Holy Spirit like a well of water within me. But I see in Your Word that there is more of Your Spirit I can receive. Just as Your disciples received the Holy Spirit on the Day of Pentecost, I desire to be filled with the Spirit so that rivers of living water can flow out of me to bless and touch others with Your love. I ask You to fill me with the Spirit right now, in Jesus' name. And as an evidence of being filled with the Spirit, I expect to speak in other tongues as Your Word declares. Amen!

In Acts chapter 2:4, it says the disciples began to speak with other tongues. *They* spoke in tongues. The Holy Spirit did not speak in tongues. They did. Neither did the Holy Spirit move their lips and tongues. They did. The disciples had to yield to the Spirit. That's what "*as the Spirit gave them utterance*" means (Acts 2:4). You too have to yield your voice to the Holy Spirit and begin to speak. If you are born again and you prayed that prayer, I encourage you to lift your hands and heart to the Lord. Thank Him for filling you with the Holy Spirit. As you run out of known words to describe your thanks and God's goodness, stop speaking in your native language and begin to speak whatever sound or syllable comes to your mind (even if it is not a sound or language you are familiar with).

God has chosen tongues to be one of the signs we are filled with the Spirit because the tongue is one of our unruliest members (James 3:8). When we yield our tongues and lips to speak a language our minds cannot control, it is a sign we are filled with the Spirit. If you asked God to fill you with the Holy Spirit by praying the above prayer, I believe you are filled with the Spirit. You have been baptized into the Spirit, and as evidence of that baptism, you will speak with a new spiritual language from God—tongues. If you have prayed and received the Holy Spirit, please contact our ministry at *info@gregmohr.com* and let us know. We would love to hear what God is doing in your life as a result of receiving the fullness of the Holy Spirit!

The Purpose of Staying Filled with the Spirit

The purpose of being filled with the Spirit and praying in other tongues is to help you stay sensitive and yielded to the Spirit. This baptism of the Holy Spirit enables you to draw out the wisdom God deposited in your born-again spirit and access the mind of Christ. But even after receiving this new dimension of the Spirit—the baptism of the Holy Spirit and speaking in other tongues—it is our choice whether we stay more filled or less filled with the Spirit.

> The purpose of being filled with the Spirit and praying in other tongues is to help you stay sensitive and yielded to the Spirit.

The following verse in Acts 4 reveals that the disciples who had already been filled with the Spirit on the Day of Pentecost were *filled again* with the Holy Spirit.

> *And when they had prayed, the place where they were assembled together was shaken; and they were all filled with the Holy Spirit, and they spoke the word of God with boldness.*
>
> Acts 4:31

119

This verse reveals to us that being filled with the Spirit is not just a one-time experience. Though it does begin there, being filled with (and staying full of) the Holy Spirit is a daily choice. It is a lifestyle of remaining yielded and sensitive to the Holy Spirit. It is a relationship. Let's look at another key passage of Scripture showing the connection between being filled with the Spirit and wisdom.

> *See then that you walk circumspectly, not as fools but as wise, redeeming the time, because the days are evil. Therefore do not be unwise, but understand what the will of the Lord is. And do not be drunk with wine, in which is dissipation; but be filled with the Spirit.*
>
> Ephesians 5:15-18

The Apostle Paul, by inspiration of the Holy Spirit, wrote this to a group of Ephesian disciples who had already received the baptism in the Holy Spirit. Acts 19 records that event. While in Ephesus, Paul asked a group of believers if they had received the Holy Spirit since they believed. The disciples responded that they had not even heard about the Holy Spirit. Paul shared this subsequent baptism into the Spirit with them, and they were all filled with the Spirit and spoke in tongues (Acts 19:1-6). Now Paul is encouraging this same group of disciples to continue to be filled with the Spirit. The literal translation here is "be being filled," which requires a lifestyle of staying full of the Spirit.

Notice that Paul also connects staying filled with the Spirit to being wise, redeeming the time, and understanding what the will of the Lord is. It takes wisdom to make the best use of our time.

It takes wisdom to understand what the will of the Lord is for our lives. According to Paul, in order for us to access the wisdom of God, it is essential we stay filled with the Spirit. Ephesians 5 goes on to address additional aspects of staying filled with the Spirit.

> *Speaking to one another in psalms and hymns and spiritual songs, singing and making melody in your heart to the Lord, giving thanks always for all things to God the Father in the name of our Lord Jesus Christ, submitting to one another in the fear of God.*
>
> Ephesians 5:19-21

Immediately after telling us to stay continually filled with the Spirit, Paul shares these verses to tell us how we are to do that. We can break this passage down into four categories of actions that help us stay full of the Holy Spirit.

1. Encouraging others in the Word and song (v. 19)
2. Singing and making melody in your heart to the Lord (v. 19)
3. Giving thanks always (v. 20)
4. Submitting to one another in the fear of the Lord (v. 21)

I want to emphasize the last two traits that assist us in staying full of the Spirit. First, "*giving thanks always.*" Another verse of Scripture that supports this idea says, "*In everything give thanks; for this is the will of God in Christ Jesus*" (1 Thessalonians 5:18). Giving thanks in the midst of everything is the will of God and releases the wisdom of God in our lives. You and I can be right in the middle of the geographic and vocational purpose of God

Being thankful in everything, not for everything, is the will of God for you and me.

for our lives yet miss His will by a million miles when we cease to be thankful. Being thankful *in* everything, not *for* everything, is the will of God for you and me.

The second trait I want to focus on is *"submitting to one another in the fear of the Lord."* True submission involves a heart that respects all authority in our life. Jesus did not use the "God card" to excuse Himself from submitting to His parents' authority, yet many Christians do this. When Jesus stayed behind at the temple and his parents came searching for Him, He could have said, "Didn't you know I must be about My Father's business? You all go home, and I will see you later." He didn't do that. The Bible tells us He went with them and was subject to, or submitted to, them. And because of that Scripture says He grew in wisdom, stature, and favor with God and man (Luke 2:51-52).

It is not possible to submit to God without submitting to the authorities He has placed in your life. Let me clarify: I am not talking about being a doormat to others or submitting to any type of abuse. If that is what you are experiencing at the hand of the authorities in your life, you need to seek help. You may need to find a way to leave that situation. But anarchy and rebellion against *all* authority is not the remedy for your experience with or abuse by authority. Rather, trusting in God and staying full of the Spirit is.

Another important truth about submission is that submission is not the same as agreement. You haven't begun to submit until you are *willing* to do what someone in authority asks of you when you do not agree or want to do it. I'm not talking about doing anything that violates the Word of God or is sin. But being *willing* to do what your flesh doesn't want is a character trait of being full of the Spirit. It is a major key in drawing on God's wisdom for your life!

> *If you are willing and obedient, you shall eat the good of the land.*
>
> Isaiah 1:19

It is not possible to submit to God without submitting to the authorities He has placed in your life.

According to this verse, our willingness is just as important as our obedience as we submit ourselves to various authorities in our lives.

Drawing up Wisdom

I want to close out this chapter by sharing with you the benefit of praying in other tongues. Look at these verses that reveal the connection between praying in your spiritual language (tongues) and accessing the wisdom of God.

> *For he who speaks in a tongue does not speak to men but to God...however, in the spirit he speaks mysteries.*
>
> 1 Corinthians 14:2

> *But we speak the wisdom of God in a mystery, the hidden wisdom which God ordained before the ages for our glory.*
>
> 1 Corinthians 2:7

By connecting these two verses, we receive a powerful revelation. When we pray in tongues we speak mysteries, and those mysteries are the wisdom of God. When we pray in the Spirit (other tongues), we draw the mind of Christ and wisdom of God up from our spirits to our minds.

When we merged our first church with another in Houston, Texas, we began praying and seeking the Lord about our next step in ministry. During that season I spent a lot of time praying in the Spirit. I started a consulting business in order to take care of my family's needs but knew that was just temporary. One day as I was praying in the Spirit, the desire to be in Houston suddenly left my heart. We had lived in Houston for twenty years, so this change in desire surprised me. But it lined up with what the Holy Spirit had shown me about Jesus moving His ministry base from Nazareth to the northern areas of Galilee and Capernaum (Matt. 4:12-13). And as I kept praying in the Spirit, I knew our next ministry assignment would be somewhere in North Texas. A few months later a door opened for us in Decatur, Texas, which is in the northern part of the state. Thank God for the baptism of the Holy Spirit and the gift of praying in tongues, which God used to direct us into this new ministry assignment.

> When we pray in the Spirit (other tongues), we draw the mind of Christ and wisdom of God up from our spirits to our minds.

God knows the plans He has for us (Jer. 29:11). He knows the assignments He has prepared for our lives, and as we pray in the Spirit, we can know and discover them too.

Now we have received, not the spirit of the world,
but the Spirit who is from God, that we might know
the things that have been freely given to us by God.

1 Corinthians 2:12

I remember Oral Roberts once sharing with a group of pastors about how the Lord gave him the plan to build Oral Roberts University. He said God gave him the land the university was to be built on, but he did not know how to do what God had put in his heart. Oral said he walked on the property and prayed in tongues for several hours. While praying, God enlightened his mind with the wisdom and understanding he needed. God showed Oral how to build the school. Oral already had this knowledge in his spirit, but he had to release it by praying in the Spirit. The same is true for you and me.

When we pray in other tongues the Bible tells us it is our spirit that is praying. When we received the Lord, we became joined to the Lord in our spirit (I Cor. 6:17). So when we are praying in tongues our spirit is praying, and we are praying the perfect will of God. Also, the wisdom of God and mind of Christ that resides in our spirit is drawn up to our mind as we pray in the Spirit. What a powerful tool we have available to us when we pray in other tongues!

Staying full of the Spirit is something available for each of us. I encourage you to walk in the revelation I have shared with you in this chapter. Stay yielded and sensitive to the Holy Spirit, and pray in the Spirit daily. Accessing the mind of Christ and walking in the wisdom of God consistently will be your reward.

Chapter 10

Live in God's Peace

Do you hear God's voice clearly? How do you know whether what you are hearing is God or just your own mind, will, or emotions? Is it possible for each born-again child of God to hear His voice and make a distinction between the flesh and the spirit? Most people's interest is piqued when addressing this aspect of the wisdom of God because we all have a desire to hear the Lord's voice clearly and with certainty. We want to make good decisions and follow His will, but how do we do that with confidence?

The Word of God clearly states that God's sheep hear His voice. They know or recognize His voice and will not follow a stranger (John 10:4-5,14, and 27). Yet many young and immature Christians have told me they heard something from God that doesn't line up with the Word of God at all. For example, a man I will call Tom from our church in North Texas once told me he was called to minister to one of the Native American tribes in New Mexico. He believed he was supposed to move there, but his wife didn't agree because he had no ability to provide for her and their children if he moved. I counseled Tom to treat his desire to minister to this particular tribe as a mission ministry. He could go there from time to time on short trips but then return home to care for his family. Rather than moving to New Mexico, I suggested he make North Texas his home base. I let Tom know that if the Lord was truly speaking to him to move to New Mexico, things would open up and the finances would come in, allowing his entire family to move there. I advised him to wait on the Lord and wait for his wife to hear from God and come into agreement with him before making any major moves.

Tom didn't like or heed my counsel at all. He came back to me and said the Lord told him to leave his wife and children so that he could fulfill the call of God on his life. He used some verses from Mark 10 to justify his decision. But I told Tom he had taken those verses out of context and completely neglected other passages of Scripture that tell us to care for our families. Let me show you what I mean:

> *Then Peter began to say to Him, "See, we have left all and followed You." So Jesus answered and said, "Assuredly, I say to you, there is no one who has left house or brothers or sisters or father or mother or wife or children or lands, for My sake and the gospel's, who shall not receive a hundredfold now in this time–houses and brothers and sisters and mothers and children and lands, with persecutions– and in the age to come, eternal life."*
>
> Mark 10:28-30

These verses in Mark do not instruct us to leave our families in order to follow Jesus. In the beginning of Mark 10, Jesus rebukes the Pharisees who wanted to use the law to leave their wives and trade them in for new models. The context of these verses is to not be frivolous regarding our family commitments. Jesus was simply responding to Peter to assure him that anything he and the disciples lost in their pursuit of Him would be restored. I told Tom there was no way what he planned to do was from God because it violated Scripture. Look at this other instruction about our responsibility to take care of our families. It cannot be clearer!

> *But if anyone does not provide for his own, and especially for those of his household, he has denied the faith and is worse than an unbeliever.*
>
> 1 Timothy 5:8

God wasn't asking Tom to leave his family or sacrifice them on the altar of ministry. Unfortunately, Tom persisted. He left his wife and family to move to New Mexico, and he and his wife eventually divorced. I don't doubt God gave Tom a desire to minister to that Native American tribe, but how Tom went about it was wrong. What Tom said God told him to do to fulfill his call did not line up with the Word.

The peace of God is our safety net. It confirms whether what we are hearing is from God or our flesh—whether it is wisdom or not.

Here's the truth my friends: The Holy Spirit will never tell you to do something that violates the written Word of God! And what God says to do will always be accompanied with peace, not confusion, emotional drama, turmoil, or strife. The peace of God is our safety net. It confirms whether what we are hearing is from God or our flesh—whether it is wisdom or not. Let's look at the following verses regarding the connection between wisdom and the peace of God.

> *But the wisdom that is from above is...peaceable.*
> James 3:17

> *Happy is the man who finds wisdom...Her ways are ways of pleasantness, and all her paths are peace.*
> Proverbs 3:13, 17

There is a strong connection between God's wisdom and peace. In fact, all the paths of wisdom are peace. Wow! When God speaks to us, it always lines up with the written Word and will always be accompanied by His peace. The reason that some believers do not hear God clearly or walk in wisdom consistently in their decision making is they don't know and value the written Word of God. They expect God to speak to them in some supernatural way, and they place greater value on the way God speaks than on making sure what they hear lines up with His Word and is accompanied by peace.

Elijah fell into this trap after Jezebel threatened to kill him. Emotionally overwrought, he fled to the wilderness to hide. After several days an angel of the Lord appeared to Elijah and fed him. Elijah then fled to Mount Horeb where God spoke to him.

> *Then He said, "Go out, and stand on the mountain before the Lord." And behold, the Lord passed by, and a great and strong wind tore into the*

mountains and broke the rocks in pieces before the LORD, but the LORD was not in the wind; and after the wind an earthquake, but the Lord was not in the earthquake; and after the earthquake a fire, but the LORD was not in the fire; and after the fire a still small voice.

1 Kings 19:11-12

After seeing fire fall from heaven to consume his burnt offering on Mount Carmel, Elijah was looking to hear from God in another supernatural and spectacular way. But God needed to teach Elijah about the primary way He speaks. Though God was in the first fire that consumed Elijah's offering, He wasn't in the strong wind on the mountain. He wasn't in the earthquake or the fire on the mountain. God spoke to Elijah in a still, small voice.

Brothers and sisters, God *can* speak to us through supernatural means such as visions, dreams, prophetic words, and open and closed doors. But those instances are rare; they are the exception rather than the rule in our walk with God. Unfortunately, like Elijah, many believers fall into this trap. They desire for God to confirm His direction in their lives with something supernatural or spectacular. Many of my prophetic friends fall into this category.

I love prophetic people. They inspire me to move into greater dimensions of operating in the gifts of the Spirit. They challenge me to stay sensitive to the move of the Spirit. Yet some of them only place value on God speaking in spectacular ways. God *can* speak to us through open and closed doors, prophetic words, an audible voice, angels, visions, and dreams, but those are not the primary ways God speaks. Expecting God to confirm His direction and wisdom with some supernatural or spectacular sign and wonder is an immature way to follow the Lord. That would be like seeking the Lord about a job and expecting Him to physically take your hand and walk you down to the specific address of the business that has an opening for your skill set and help you fill out the application. This is, in effect, what we are doing when we seek God for His will but refuse to step out on that still, small voice or impression in our spirits. Like a child, we want God to confirm that we are hearing the still, small voice correctly by sending us a sign or wonder that leaves no doubt the impression we received is from the Lord.

Not only is this immature, but it also sets us up for deception. The enemy can open and close doors, appear as an angel of light, or send some other voice to get our attention. But he cannot counterfeit God's Word. The Lord has spoken to me by supernatural means in the past. I once had an angel get in my car and speak to me. I have also had visions and dreams. God has directed me with open and closed doors of opportunity. But these instances do not dominate my life or walk with God. They are the exceptions rather than the rule. They are not the primary ways God speaks to you and me.

> The more yielded we are to the Spirit, the more apt we are to recognize and be responsive to His still, small voice within us.

If you want to walk in wisdom and make good decisions in your life on a consistent basis, choose to value the Word of God. Choose to follow the peace of God above any other supernatural means of confirmation. The primary way God speaks to us is with an inward witness or, as First Kings calls it, the "still, small voice." This "voice" originates inside us. It is not a spectacular outward demonstration of power. This is why the principle I shared in the previous chapter about staying full of the Spirit is so important. The more yielded we are to the Spirit, the more apt we are to recognize and be responsive to His still, small voice within us.

In my experience and walk with the Lord, the still, small voice of God typically comes to me in the form of a strong inward impression or desire the Lord plants in my heart. This inward witness and desire always lines up with God's Word and is accompanied by His peace. It is a much more reliable way of recognizing and following God's voice than waiting for an opened or closed door. It's more consistent than someone giving you a prophetic word or you receiving a vision or dream. Even if you do receive one of these "more supernatural" confirmations of God's will, it is still necessary to check them out with the Word, God's peace, the witness of your spirit, and godly counsel.

The following verse from the book of Psalms provides us with a picture of the Lord's voice and leading in our lives.

> *Delight yourself also in the* Lord, *and He shall give you the desires of your heart.*
> Psalm 37:4

This verse is not saying God will give us the selfish desires of our flesh. The word "*delight*" in this verse means to be pliable or to yield. This verse says that as we yield ourselves to the Lord and seek Him by setting aside our own plans and agendas—by being pliable—we will discover or discern the desires of our hearts that were planted there by God. Any desire God has planted in our hearts is the will of God for our lives. Instead of following after prophetic words, visions, dreams, and open or closed doors, we should be seeking God to discover what desires He has already planted in our hearts. This is a much more consistent and surer way of being led by the Spirit and walking in wisdom in our lives.

Praying, but Hearing "Nothing"

While I pastored the church in Decatur, Texas, the board and I were praying and seeking the Lord about purchasing additional land on which to build. We were landlocked in our present location, with less than three acres of property and no more room to expand. The mayor of our town was a real estate agent, and I happened to mention to him what we wanted to do. He had recently listed a piece of property on one of the main roads in our town that met our needs. Long story short, we ended up purchasing twenty-three acres on that road for just $232,000! The woman who sold us the property was a former kindergarten teacher. When she heard about our vision to reach the children and youth of our area, she gave us a steal of a deal. Three years later, someone offered us $300,000 for three acres of our twenty-three-acre property. Our property was adjacent to the new hospital, so its value had gone up significantly. We accepted this offer, paid off our new land, and still had twenty acres to build on in the future, free and clear. Only God's favor and walking in wisdom by following the desires He placed in our hearts could have achieved that deal!

We saved money for several years in preparation for building on that land. Then, five years after selling off a portion of it, we were presented with another possible God-opportunity. We had not yet started to build on this property because changes to our plans, increased building costs, and city code issues had doubled the cost of our original bid. At the time, we were not comfortable borrowing that much money. While seeking God about what to do (build a smaller initial building that could be expanded upon or commit to borrowing more money), a real estate broker came to us with an offer to purchase our remaining twenty acres. The offer: $1.8 million. Wow! What an increase! Our property value had appreciated over 8 times what we paid for it eight years previously.

So, the dilemma presented to our leadership team was, "Do we sell this land now? Or keep it to build on later?" You would think that would be an easy decision, but it wasn't. It wasn't our property. That land belonged to the Lord and His church; we were simply the stewards of it. As stewards, we wanted to know His will regarding this decision, not our own. Our leadership team discussed the options, but we didn't have a clear consensus among us. They said they would pray and seek God with me about this decision, but they also said they felt strongly that the Lord would speak to me about what to do since I was the one He spoke to about purchasing the property eight years before.

I was thankful for their trust in me, but making a 1.8-million-dollar decision was not something we could afford to miss God's leading on. Since we were supposed to respond to the real estate broker within seven days, I felt the weight of this decision looming. So, I did what I knew to do. I spent that time seeking the Lord and delighting myself in Him. I set aside my own preferences so that I could hear His will. I spent extra time in the Word, positioning myself to allow His Word to make a distinction between the desires in my spirit and those in my soul (Heb. 4:12). I sought godly counsel from other pastors and leaders I trusted. And I spent a lot of time praying in the Spirit. But I sensed no clear-cut direction from the Lord.

That week, I listened to several teachers on the radio and watched preachers on television. It seemed like each one was sharing about how they were clearly hearing God speak to them. I was praying. I was seeking God and spending extra time in His Word. I was seeking counsel, and I was hearing nothing. Nada. Zilch.

The day before we were to let the real estate broker know of our decision, I scheduled a meeting with our elders. That morning I drove to our twenty acres, parked my car in an adjacent parking lot, and prayed. I poured my heart out to the Lord, reminding Him of everything I'd been struggling with in my mind and of my desire for His will to be done instead of mine. I told Him that I knew He knew my heart, but that I wanted to know His and, so far, I had heard nothing. I prayed in the Spirit for a good while and reminded God that I needed to let my elders know my recommendation that night so that we could tell the broker the next day (as if He didn't know). After praying everything I knew to pray, I got quiet for a few minutes. During the silence I heard the Lord ask me several questions.

He said, "Son, have you been seeking and delighting yourself in Me by setting aside your personal preference about this decision?"

"Yes, Lord," I answered Him. "You know I have."

"Have you spent time in My Word," He asked, "to position yourself to allow My Word to separate the desires of your soul from the desires in your spirit?"

"Yes, Lord," I responded. "You know I have."

He went on to ask, "Have you spent time praying in the Spirit to draw My wisdom out of your spirit and into your mind?"

I responded again, "Yes, Father, You know I have."

"Have you sought godly counsel about this decision?"

"Yes, Lord, You know I have," I said again.

"Have you heard anything from Me about this decision?" He asked.

"No, Lord," I said. "You know I haven't!" Yet He *was* speaking to me at the time, presenting me with all those questions.

And then God spoke something so clearly to my heart. He said, "Son, when you seek Me, set aside your personal preferences, spend time in My Word, pray in the Spirit, and seek godly counsel and you still haven't heard anything specific from Me, it's because you don't have to. You already have My mind on the matter. Go with the strongest desire in your heart and let peace be your umpire in the process. I trust you to make this decision."

That was so powerful! I'd never heard anything so life changing in my pursuit of God's will. It brought such freedom that day to my understanding of hearing God's voice and following His will more accurately. "Really?" I responded. "You mean I don't have to hear something supernatural to confirm that what's in my heart is the right thing to do? Since I already have the mind of Christ, I just need to trust that and go with what I feel best about? It's ok to follow my strongest desire? And know that is your will?"

"Yes," He said. "And know that I have given you My peace to confirm it."

At that moment, I started praising God because I knew what I wanted to do. I wanted to sell that property and pay off the new youth building we had built. I wanted to sow into other ministries and purchase another piece of property in the area that our church could later build on. So, that is exactly what we did. I shared what God had spoken to me that morning with my elders that evening, and it all bore witness with them. We sold the property, tithed on the profit to several other ministries, and paid off the $600,000 debt on our youth building. Then we purchased nineteen acres on a major highway with the remainder of the money, and our church came out debt free!

God helped us receive this amazing deal by teaching me to trust the desires He planted in my heart just as if He spoke audibly or in some other supernatural way to me. Since that time, I have discovered this inward witness or "knowing" is the primary way God speaks to and leads each of us. This understanding has helped me become more consistent and confident in my decision making. Most of the time, if I haven't heard anything specific after seeking the Lord, setting aside my own preferences, praying in the Spirit, spending time in His Word, and seeking counsel, I just follow what I want to do or don't want to do in my heart. Then His peace becomes my safety net. It protects me and helps me change direction if, for some reason, I have missed it.

> *And let the peace of God rule* [umpire] *in your hearts.*
>
> Colossians 3:15

The word "*rule*" in this verse means to govern, decide, arbitrate, direct and to be an umpire. In baseball, the umpire rules. They call the balls and strikes for batters and decide whether a player is safe or out when running the bases. The Holy Spirit, through the Apostle Paul, tells us that peace is our umpire in finding and following God's will. We can use peace to monitor whether we are safe or heading out of bounds, in or out of the will of God. Have you ever been in a place you knew you weren't supposed to be? Have you ever been with an individual or group of people you didn't have peace about? That is wisdom calling out to you. That is God directing you through peace.

God's GPS System

The stronger the peace you have about something, the more certain you can be it is the will of God. The less peace you have, the more certain you can be it is not the will of God. You cannot miss the will of God if you don't want to.

The Holy Spirit is not as rigid nor the will of God as static as some have believed and taught. Do you have a smartphone lady who can speak to and direct you? All you have to do is ask a question or type in an address. What happens when following her road directions, if you make a wrong turn? She speaks to you more sternly and tells you to make a U-turn. If you continue on the wrong course, she will get quiet for a moment and then recalibrate a new course to get you back on track. Brothers and sisters, your smartphone lady is not smarter than the Holy Spirit! If your smartphone lady can do that, consider what the Holy Spirit can do if you miss a turn in

You cannot miss the will of God if you don't want to.

> Follow peace. If you make a wrong turn in pursuing God's will for your life, He can recalibrate and get you back on course!

your pursuit of the will and wisdom of God? If you are yielded and sensitive to Him by staying full of the Spirit, He will nudge and direct you with His peace.

Most of the time, we discover God's wisdom and will for our lives by following the witness in our spirits. That witness manifests itself as a strong desire accompanied by peace and is the primary way God leads us. Follow peace. If you make a wrong turn in pursuing God's will for your life, He can recalibrate and get you back on course! Even when God does lead us through something more "supernatural" like a vision, dream, prophetic word, or audible voice, His accompanying peace (or the lack of it) is our safeguard. Following His peace is the safety net God has given us to confirm that we are walking in His will and wisdom for our lives.

Chapter 11

Receiving Correction

Becoming disciples of Jesus who walk in wisdom and raise up other disciples, including our own children, starts by modeling and walking in the principles I have shared in this book. It continues by developing a willingness to receive correction and by administering appropriate correction to those with whom you are in relationship like your children.

Some parents I know, even Christian parents, have believed a lie that correction will hurt their child's self-image. And while I agree that punishment can hurt a child, biblical correction will not harm your children or others; rather, it will help them become wise. Other parents' false understanding of grace means there are no consequences for sin. They say we are supposed to walk in mercy and love regardless of someone's actions. Yet the love of God can only operate in truth. Children need boundaries and consequences for violating those boundaries in life, or their flesh will rule their decisions. Children who grow up with no boundaries and no correction grow up rebellious and without wisdom. Proverbs

29:15 says, *"The rod and rebuke give wisdom, but a child left to himself brings shame to his mother."* Here is a powerful truth: biblical correction brings wisdom.

When correcting children, it is not appropriate to attack who they are as a person. Don't tell them "You are a bad boy" or "You are a bad girl." Don't speak lack over them, saying "You're stupid" or "You're a slow learner" or "You're rebellious" or "You'll never amount to anything." These types of statements can wound a child and eventually redefine their God-given identity. The wise way to correct our children is to attack their behavior, not their person. Tell them what they did was wrong and why it was wrong. Show them how their actions hurt someone else and give them appropriate consequences for their actions. Then remind them of who they are. Leave them with hope. Tell them "But you are better than that!" and point them toward who they are in Christ. Remind them of their ability to walk in love and the choice they have to live from their spirit rather than their flesh. Remember: Punishment is something done to the child. Correction is something done for the child.

> Punishment is something done to the child. Correction is something done for the child.

The verse we just read in Proverbs 29 says both the rod and rebuke are appropriate methods of correction. Each can give your children wisdom. The word translated *"rod"* here is literally a switch or small stick used in spanking a child. The word *"rebuke"* means an argument, reasoning, or action appropriate for bringing about correction. When my children were young, we found long, thin dowel rods at the hardware store and used them for spanking when they knowingly and willfully disobeyed. These dowel rods were very small in diameter and would break with a small amount of force. But they stung like fire. As our children grew, we transitioned to the use of the "rebuke."

Years ago, when my daughter was young, she did something wrong that deserved a spanking. When I asked her to lean over the bed, she turned around and said, "But it will hurt, Daddy!"

"Yes, sweetheart," I said. "It is intended to hurt. This will help you remember that there are consequences for your actions."

For those who live in a state or country where spanking is forbidden, it is still your responsibility to correct your children as part of the discipleship process of raising wise sons and daughters. But let me encourage you, you still have leverage. There are other disciplinary options. One that Janice and I used many times came from the words of Jesus.

> *Whoever seeks to save his life will lose it, and whoever loses his life will preserve it.*
>
> Luke 17:33

As our children grew older, we applied this principle to their correction like this: whatever you seek to save through disobedience, you lose. We made it a priority to know what each of our children valued most. Then whenever they willfully violated a boundary, they lost something of value for a period of time. The principle works very well as a deterrent to bad behavior or the mistreatment of others (especially siblings). For example, if your son or daughter loves to spend time playing games on their smartphone or electronic tablet and they willfully disobey or violate a clear boundary you have set, remove their smartphone or electronic tablet for one to three days, depending on the degree of violation. However, you should be careful about grounding your children for longer than a week or threatening to keep their phone for an extended period. Something may come up where you need them to join the family on an outing or have their phone available, and then you will have to relent on your word. Correction doesn't work if you fail to follow through.

Arbuckle Wilderness

Several years ago, our family traveled from North Texas to Tulsa, Oklahoma for a conference and some vacation time. On the way home we stopped at Arbuckle Wilderness in southern Oklahoma. On one side of the wilderness park was a water park with slides and a swimming area that looked like a lot of fun for children. On the other side was a drive-through animal kingdom with all types of unique animals we could see and take pictures of. Our two older children wanted to go to the water park, but the two younger children wanted to see the animals. We only had time for one of these attractions, so I encouraged the children to come to a consensus. After fifteen to twenty minutes of arguing, they still could not make a decision. So, instead of enjoying part of the Arbuckle Wilderness, they enjoyed none of it.

As our children climbed into the car, I told them that since they were unwilling to give up their preference for one another, we were going home to do chores. What they sought to save, they lost. And they spent the rest of the day pulling weeds in our yard at home. My children are adults now, yet any mention of Arbuckle

Wilderness brings up a memory and important lesson none of them have forgotten.

There are other important principles I have learned regarding appropriate and inappropriate correction of children. First, it is not effective to correct our children when we are angry. That will frustrate them. The only person we need to count to ten for is ourselves. It is important to wait to administer correction until our emotions are under control. Next, we should not train our children to respond to us by raising our voices or using their middle names. Rather, we should train them to simply obey our word and listen to us the first time.

> *And you, fathers, do not provoke your children to wrath, but bring them up in the training and admonition of the Lord.*
>
> Ephesians 6:4

Third, putting children in "time out" with their noses in a corner breeds contempt and anger. They will just sit there fuming and embarrassed. We can give them a time-out from video games or one of their digital gadgets, but making them sit on a "dunce" stool in a corner encourages them to become angrier and more disrespectful toward us. Next, we should only correct our children for crossing a clear boundary we have communicated with them or for showing disrespect toward us or someone else. It is not necessary to correct them for childish mistakes, such as spilling their milk or some other accident.

As parents, my wife and I put a few other things in place that helped strengthen our relationship with our children and motivated them in positive ways. First, we determined that nothing our children did would shame us. Jesus is not ashamed to call us His brothers (Heb. 2:11), and even as adults, we have made our share of mistakes. We did not allow what our children did or didn't do to define our success as parents. This understanding helped us take the focus off ourselves when our children made mistakes, and reminded us that all correction was about our children learning to walk in wisdom and to grow and mature. It wasn't about our image.

We also made ourselves available to our children anytime they needed us. We didn't require them to compete with our careers or ministry. We allowed them to interrupt a meeting or phone call anytime they needed us. This paid off big time in keeping our relationship with them strong, especially when they needed to talk or open up with us. These things helped us develop a healthy family culture that included the right balance of love and discipline and helped us raise wise children who value their parents' instruction.

> *A wise son heeds his father's instruction, but a scoffer does not listen to rebuke.*
>
> Proverbs 13:1

Correction or Rejection?

Even as adults, we need to stay open to correction if we are going to grow in maturity and learn to walk in God's wisdom and will for our lives. The issue is about pride versus humility. According to James 4:6, God resists the proud but gives more grace (including wisdom) to the humble. A proud person does not respond correctly to instruction. They say, "I know, I know." But they don't know. Either what they know is not enough to be successful in the situation they are facing, or they aren't acting on what they know. In either case, pride hinders them from drawing on the wisdom God has made available to them.

> *He who keeps instruction is in the way of life, but*
> *he who refuses correction goes astray.*
>
> Proverbs 10:17

On the other hand, a humble person is teachable. They will listen to instruction and receive correction without taking it as a personal rejection. When someone who cares about us gives instruction or correction, it has the power to cause us to grow in maturity and wisdom if we will respond to it correctly. The correct response to any instruction or correction should be openness and humility.

The correct response to any instruction or correction should be openness and humility.

My first response to anyone trying to help me through correction is being willing to examine my heart and actions to discover if what they are pointing out is true. Even if their perspective of my situation is limited, biased, or one-sided, I can still learn and grow by asking the Lord if there is truth or facts regarding what they have shared with me. Rather than allowing myself to become defensive, I have learned to listen when someone feels strongly enough to share instruction or correction with me. I then take it to the Lord to find out if I need to repent or change something.

In one of my first ministry assignments, I learned the value of receiving correction without taking it personally. When you take correction personally, it feels like rejection. While attending a conference sponsored by one of our sister churches in Houston, Texas, Bill Wilson—the children's ministry and bus pastor for Tommy Barnett's church in Davenport, Iowa spoke. Bill's sessions got my attention. I was born in Davenport, and to hear about a life-giving church there that was reaching souls and making disciples for Jesus was exciting to me. But most importantly, Bill Wilson shared how, through their bus ministry, they were bringing hundreds of children and youth to Jesus. I got all excited and took a trip to see their bus and children's ministry in action. Being immersed in their vision imparted great vision to me.

When we returned home, I spent time praying and making plans to implement a bus and children's ministry in our church. I set up a meeting with our pastor to share the vision and request that they consider purchasing a bus for that purpose. I also volunteered to oversee this new ministry.

At first, the church board was not open to making such a large investment in an unproven ministry. But I felt God was leading me in that direction, so I asked if we could start the ministry if I bought the bus. The board approved my plan, so we bought our first bus. That Sunday we brought seventeen children to church. The next Sunday we brought forty-two children to church and the children's church leader quit. So, my wife and I became the children's pastors by default.

As the ministry grew, we saw children born again, healed, and filled with the Spirit each Sunday. Our pastor became so excited about this outreach that he convinced the board to purchase another bus. One Sunday, we bused over 150 children to church in a church of only 400 adults! Before the bus ministry started, we only had 25 children in the children's church. During that time, some of the board members came to me complaining about a small oil leak in one of the buses. They felt it was ruining the parking lot. Others were not happy about the increased cleaning costs the church was incurring due to the additional children and the larger space requirements. I was not happy about their complaints. I felt they were being petty considering the number of changed lives we were seeing because of the bus and children's ministry. I told a few members of my team what was being said, including some judgmental statements of my own. This got back to our pastor, and he called me into his office to ask if the complaining and murmuring he'd heard about was true. I acknowledged that it was and apologized to him and later to my team. Though I still thought these board members' priorities were out of order, it was not my place to speak negatively of them and share that judgment with my team members.

I learned an important lesson that day through my pastor's correction. Even if I think I am right about a situation, it is not appropriate to share my problems with another church member or leader. If I have a problem with someone, I need to take it to them directly. Though uncomfortable at the time, my pastor's leadership brought wisdom and maturity to me.

The Importance of Accountability

Each of us needs correction because each of us has blind spots. We don't always see what we are doing wrong, even when it is hurtful to someone we love. Because of this truth, I developed a habit of voluntarily asking friends and mentors to speak into my life about anything they see in my words, actions, or attitude toward others that is un-Christlike.

Paul Milligan, a good friend of mine and one-time elder of my church, was one of those individuals. Years ago, I gave him permission to share anything he saw in my life that did not represent the Lord or edify others. He asked me to do the same with him. One year, we invited Paul and his wife Patsy to attend Andrew Wommack's ministers' conference with us. At this time, Andrew held the conference in the beautiful mountain town of Buena Vista, Colorado. Paul, Patsy, Janice, and I shared a two-bedroom condo for the week and had a wonderful time in worship, receiving the ministry of the Word, and fellowship with other pastors and ministers. A week after we returned home, Paul asked if he could meet with me.

Paul shared that while we were at the ministers' conference, he noticed a number of times I corrected my wife. She would be telling a story, and I'd interrupt to correct her about details that didn't really matter or affect the story. Her stories were true, but the details were inaccurate. Paul said, "I know you aren't aware you are doing that, Greg, but you are unintentionally shutting your wife down." Initially I was surprised by what he said. I was not aware I had been doing that, but the more I reflected on his correction, I knew he was right. I was shutting my wife down by correcting her over and over again.

I was devastated to realize I had been doing that. I thanked Paul for telling me and went home to apologize to my wife.

She appreciated my apology and told me that Paul was right. I received correction through my friend that helped me serve, love, and release my wife, instead of quenching and shutting her down. Thank God for godly correction through our friends!

> *Faithful are the wounds of a friend, but the kisses of an enemy are deceitful.*
>
> Proverbs 27:6

We can see this same principle of correction being applied in the New Testament. When Peter and the leaders of the church in Jerusalem refused to eat with the Gentiles in Antioch, Paul corrected them.

> *Now when Peter had come to Antioch, I withstood him to his face, because he was to be blamed; for before certain men came from James, he would eat with the Gentiles; but when they came, he withdrew and separated himself, fearing those who were of the circumcision. And the rest of the Jews also played the hypocrite with him, so that even Barnabas was carried away with their hypocrisy.*
>
> Galatians 2:11-13

Peter and Barnabas were modeling a mixture of law and grace to the Jews that came from Jerusalem and the Gentile believers of Antioch. The Jews were unconsciously holding on to some remnants of law-keeping from their religious lives before Christ, and Paul brought some much needed correction to them in this situation. Jesus did something similar when correcting the Pharisees, but they did not receive it as well. Thankfully, Peter had learned his lesson on staying teachable and responded correctly to Paul's rebuke.

Earlier in Peter's life, when Jesus corrected him in Matthew chapter 16 he did not respond so well. Immediately following Peter's revelation and confession of Jesus as the Christ, he stuck his foot in his mouth—big time! Jesus told the disciples not to tell anyone He was the Christ and then began sharing that He must go to Jerusalem to suffer at the hands of the elders and chief priests. He told them He would be crucified and then raised from the dead. Following this, Peter rebuked Jesus and got that rebuke turned back on himself.

If we are going to grow in wisdom and maturity, it is essential for us to remain open to correction from the Lord, directly and through others.

Then Peter took Him aside and began to rebuke Him, saying, "Far be it from You, Lord; this shall not happen to You!" But He [Jesus] turned and said to Peter, "Get behind Me, Satan! You are an offense to Me, for you are not mindful of the things of God, but the things of men."

Matthew 16:22-23

No doubt that was difficult for Peter to hear! Can you imagine what Peter felt like? Jesus had just commended Peter for recognizing and acknowledging Him as the Christ, and then He turned around and called Peter satan! Peter was yielding to satan with his words, and Jesus called him out on it. It was an important lesson for Peter to learn, but it is also an important lesson for all Jesus' disciples to learn. We must learn to speak the truth in love to one another, especially when someone speaks something contrary to the Word, as Peter did.

If we are going to grow in wisdom and maturity, it is essential for us to remain open to correction from the Lord, directly and through others. Let's look at the following passage of Scripture from Hebrews chapter 12 that emphasizes this principle. When reading these verses, please note the word "*chastening*" means correction.

> *If you endure chastening, God deals with you as with sons; for what son is there whom a father does not chasten? But if you are without chastening, of which all have become partakers, then you are illegitimate and not sons, ... Now no chastening seems to be joyful for the present, but painful; nevertheless, afterward it yields the peaceable fruit of righteousness to those who have been trained by it.*
>
> Hebrews 12:7-8, 11

The primary way God corrects us is through His Word. He doesn't use sickness, disease, pain, troubles, or trials to correct His children as some have taught. In other words, satan is not God's spanking board! Certainly, we can learn and receive from the Lord whenever we go through difficult times, but people confuse those times with things God uses to teach us. Just because someone turns to the Lord in the midst of tragedy, sickness, or loss does not mean those things came from God. The Lord can use anything, even the things the enemy meant for evil, and turn it around for our good. But He is not the author of evil. He does not send bad things to teach us something. He teaches us through His Word.

As we finish this chapter, let me share an example with you of how the Lord brought me correction. When I served as pastor in our church in Decatur, Texas, I received a call from a well-known television evangelist who planned to be in our area and wanted to know if he could minister at our church. The date he wanted to come was open, so I let him know we would be thrilled to have him. We prepared the overflow areas that opened up to our auditorium in anticipation of a larger-than-normal crowd. We spent quite a bit of money and time on advertising to let people in our area know about the event. And I found myself praying during that time for the Lord to bring in people to fill up the church for this meeting.

It seemed like we were building quite a buzz in the church and community with the news of this famous evangelist coming to a relatively small town. We could accommodate close to 500 people by using our overflow areas, so while I prayed for God to fill it up, I also prayed that the evangelist would receive a good offering. I wanted the evangelist to be impressed with our church so that he would consider coming again and would be encouraged to go to other churches in smaller communities in the future.

While I was praying these things, I heard the Lord ask, "What are you doing? Why are you praying like that?"

I responded, "Lord, You know."

Then I heard Him firmly say, "Stop it. Stop focusing on the evangelist and prostituting my bride by a one-night stand with him. This is not about the evangelist. Any meeting you host must be first about My church. You simply pray the evangelist will hear from Me and have something to minister to My people. I will take care of the evangelist!"

Whoa! I had never heard anything like that before. But I received this correction from the Lord, and it has since helped me keep my priorities in line when it comes to having guest speakers in the church. I had unconsciously allowed my focus to shift off the church and onto this evangelist. I made the adjustment so that I could better represent Jesus as the Good Shepherd of His flock. That correction changed my priorities and made me a better pastor. By the way, we had a great meeting with that evangelist. Close to 500 people attended the meetings, and many were saved and healed. And we were able to bless the evangelist as well.

Receiving correction helps both children and adults mature and grow in wisdom. A verse from the book of Proverbs says, "*The ear that hears the rebukes of life will abide among the wise*" (Prov. 15:31). One way to appropriate the wisdom God deposited in our spirits when we received Jesus as Lord is to be open to receiving correction. Biblical correction is given to us to help us grow. But we cannot benefit from it if we take it as personal rejection. Don't become defensive when others bring you correction. That is an indication of your insecurity and pride. Pride will limit the amount of wisdom you can access because God resists the proud (1 Pet. 5:5-6). Pray this with me:

> *Lord, I humble myself to receive correction by anyone You want to use to help me grow and mature. I refuse to be defensive or take correction as personal rejection. I choose to respond correctly to correction, and I expect to grow in wisdom as a result, in Jesus' name!*

Chapter 12

Develop a Great Commission Vision

In the final chapter of this book, *Walking in Wisdom*, I want to share a principle with you that most don't consider when appropriating God's wisdom. I call it "developing a Great Commission vision." The foundational verse for this principle is found in Proverbs.

> *The fruit of the righteous is a tree of life, and he*
> *who wins souls is wise.*
>
> Proverbs 11:30

As we make ourselves available to the Holy Spirit to win people to Jesus and make disciples, the innovation and creativity of the Spirit is made available to us. In the Hebrew language, the word "wins" in this verse of Proverbs means to accept, bring, buy, take from, take out, receive, marry, and carry away. This word describes the entire process of leading people to Jesus. As soul winners, we are literally taking people out of darkness and bringing them into the light. We are receiving them into the local church family and discipling them in the faith. This requires a dimension of God's wisdom that is reserved for those who make winning souls and making disciples a priority. I have experienced this wisdom both personally and corporately in ministries and churches with a Great Commission vision.

I have discovered if you will pray over your family, your neighbors, and your community, God will give you specific wisdom strategies to reach them. It doesn't matter where you live—this principle will work in any village, town, city, state, or country. It will work for any individual or family. No place or person is too hard for the power of the Gospel to reach, for the wisdom of God is greater than any deceptive plan of the enemy. And His influence in someone's life is far more powerful than any negative or evil influence.

> No place or person is too hard for the power of the Gospel to reach.

God will make wise kingdom strategies available to us to reach the individuals, families, or communities He has placed on our hearts. I first discovered this principle for accessing God's wisdom soon after I was filled with the Spirit and moved to a Spirit-filled church. I began seeking God's plan and purpose for my life and met a man in our church who led a small group of believers that met every Friday evening to witness to people on the streets of downtown Houston. I started going to witness with this group because I wanted to make a difference in my community. As a group, we would meet together at a park to pray and then drive to the downtown area of Houston and walk the streets. We handed out Gospel tracts and prayed for and ministered to the people we met. Typically three to five of us joined the group each Friday night, and we always saw people saved, healed, or recommit their lives to Christ. As I remember it, the lowest number of people we saw who accepted the Lord was four, and the highest was twenty-five in one night of ministry.

I had never done anything like that before and found it to be a powerful ministry. I also found that God's promise of increased wisdom for those who win souls to be true. One evening, about four months after becoming involved, I walked up to a young man and attempted to hand him a Gospel tract. I wanted to ask him if he knew that God loved him and had a good plan for his life, but before I could speak with him, he jumped on one of the Houston city buses. I was a little disappointed and stopped to pray, "Lord, I wish I had been able to share the Gospel with that young man."

Immediately, the Lord answered me, "That bus can share the Gospel with him and multitudes of others."

The moment the Lord spoke, I looked inside the windows of the bus that was pulling away and saw advertising banners all along its inside and top. I noticed one of the banners had a "Free! Take one" card people could pull down and take with them. In that moment God's wisdom came to me. I knew how we could reach more people with the Gospel and how we could reach them every day, not just on Friday evenings.

I met with our team and shared my idea with them. They were all excited, but our team leader wanted me to take the initiative on setting this idea in motion since God had given it to me. I prayed over it and made an appointment with the Houston Metro City bus company. I asked what it would cost to put a banner with pull-down tracts in their buses. I believe the man I spoke with was a Christian because I found great favor with him. He said that since we were a nonprofit ministry, he would give us a banner with pull down tracts in 360 Houston buses at no cost for six months! Overwhelmed at God's goodness, I thanked the man and left.

The next time I met with our team, we decided on a design for the banners. Our design asked the question, "Which way are you headed?" Then we wrote our own tracts, which included a "We Care" phone line, and met with a local printer. They gave us an amazing deal, and for six months, our banners shared the Gospel with travelers in 360 Houston buses! We saw hundreds of people come to the Lord through that God-idea; as a result, several new people became involved with our Friday night ministry.

This was my first experience accessing God's wisdom to reach people in new ways. But it came to me because I was already involved in winning souls. The point is, if we want to appropriate this dimension of God's wisdom, we must be available and involved with reaching, touching, and ministering to people.

In the last chapter, I shared about the bus and children's ministry we started in one of our churches. When we started that bus ministry, our church only averaged 25 children in children's church per week. That was a small percentage for a church of 400 people. After we purchased the second bus, we averaged over 100 children in children's church each Sunday. After a time, our church began to grow. Many of those children's parents started coming to church with their kids, received the Lord, and became disciples of Jesus! Praise God! Years later, when my wife and I returned to visit, several adults came up to us, saying, "We know the Lord and are here today because you brought us to children's church in one of those buses." They had grown up but had not forgotten how they came to know the Lord. Thank God for that wisdom strategy!

Reaching Our Community through Unity

When we moved to Decatur, Texas to pastor our second church, God put it in my heart to reach out to some of the pastors in the area for the purpose of fellowship, prayer, and reaching our community. I had read the words of Jesus in John 17 and been convinced of the effectiveness of unity among spiritual leaders. I believe unity in a community causes people in that community to come to the Lord in greater numbers.

> *I do not pray for these alone, but also for those who will believe in Me through their word; that they all may be one, as You, Father, are in Me and I in You; that they also may be one in Us, that the world may believe that You sent Me. ... I in them, and You in Me; that they may be made perfect in one, and that the world may know that You have sent Me, and have loved them as You have loved Me.*
>
> John 17:20-21, 23

This powerful passage of Scripture quotes Jesus as saying the unity of the church, especially among church leaders, increases the world's ability to believe. And it also causes them to believe the Father sent Jesus and to know and understand His love for them. I had never heard anyone teach this in all my years as a Christian. But it is Jesus speaking—in red letters. It is truth. And it is a prayer,

I believe, Jesus will see answered. Once I saw and understood this truth, I determined to be part of that answer in whatever community I served.

I met with a couple pastors in our community for coffee and fellowship, and I shared this truth with them. It blessed and motivated them to continue to meet and invite other pastors and leaders to join us. We met at least twice per month for fellowship and prayer, and over time, our group increased. We only had two conditions for those who wanted to be part of this pastors' group in our community. The first was a commitment to our faith in the virgin birth; in the sinless life, death, burial, and resurrection of Jesus; and that His shed blood was the only means for our salvation. The second condition was that each of us commit not to debate with one another over the gifts of the Spirit, tongues, healing, eschatology (end times), or our authority as a believers. This commitment went further than that because we determined not to argue over any doctrine. Each of us could share what we believed about a topic, but it was never to come to the point of debate or argument. This worked very well and brought many pastors together from different denominations in our county, including Baptists, Methodists, Church of Christ, Episcopalians, Catholics, Assembly of God, Pentecostals, and independent churches. Many close relationships were developed from this group, and many are still some of my best friends to this day.

Together, we discovered we didn't have as many differences as we had previously thought. And we found that each of us was dealing with similar challenges and problems. As we continued to meet, God started giving us wisdom about ways we could reach the community together. We started an annual, week-long revival that moved host churches every evening. Each host church pastor asked a pastor from another church in our group to speak the night the revival moved to their church. We saw the body of Christ come together during these meetings; many people were healed, and other lasting kingdom relationships were established in our community.

Our pastors' group also provided leadership for community-wide prayer meetings. One of those was held at the civic center in Decatur right after 9/11. Over 500 people attended. We held another prayer meeting right after our local elections. We invited all the local elected officials to this meeting and assigned a different pastor to pray for each one. Twenty-one of our civic leaders attended this prayer meeting as well as hundreds of people from different churches in our community. Two of the officials who attended this prayer meeting, our county sheriff and district attorney, had previously been openly critical of the other through the local media. They happened to sit next to each other at this meeting, and afterward we noticed how their animosity toward one another subsided. Their relationship became much more amiable, and the community benefited from it.

This pastors' group also did several outreaches together. One was a ministry we brought in called *Heaven's Gates & Hell's Flames*. It was an evangelistic drama of heaven and hell. The team used cast members from several churches represented in our pastors' group, and we saw hundreds of people saved in the four years we participated. So much good came from the unity of our pastors and leaders. God's wisdom was released to us, and we became a part of the answer to Jesus' prayer in John 17. The world knew that we were His disciples and that He loved them. And the kingdom was advanced in our community.

Reaching Children and Youth

As the elders and I sought the Lord about how to reach our community with the Gospel in other ways, God gave us a vision to target children and youth. We hired a children's pastor and youth pastor to do that, and they helped us develop strategies to reach and disciple the children and youth in our area. Our children's pastor held several week-long crusades each year that were very successful in reaching the children and families in our community. He also started a bus ministry using our church vans to bring children to church on Sunday mornings. I regularly encouraged our leaders to seek the Lord at the end of each calendar year about creative ways to reach more people in the year to come.

One year, my children's pastor came to me with an idea I was not initially excited about. He said God spoke to him about doing a community-wide Easter egg hunt. My first response was, "We don't believe in the Easter Bunny and don't want to endorse something that promotes an imaginary character." But then he explained to me the vision God had given him, and I warmed up to this idea.

He said people in the world would come to a free Easter egg hunt just for something fun to do with their family. He planned to print out flyers and distribute them to ten elementary schools in our county and ask local merchants for donations of bicycles, video games, gift cards, skateboards, inline skates, and toys as prizes for those who came. They planned to put slips of paper with names of specific prizes in various plastic eggs among the 20,000 he would order for this hunt. In the eggs with no prizes, he would put candy and other small items children would enjoy.

He said they would not say anything about an Easter Bunny, but rather present the Gospel to those who came. He knew of a ministry with a huge trailer and sound system we could borrow and planned to turn the trailer into a stage displaying some of the larger prizes. They would share the true meaning of Easter—the death, burial, and resurrection of Jesus—and give an invitation for salvation to the audience before the Easter egg hunt started. He envisioned holding the Easter egg hunt on our vacant twenty acres that had not yet sold and planned to rope off different sections of our property for various age groups to hunt.

I appreciated that he came to me with such a clear, complete plan and prayed over it before sharing it with our elders. We had money in our outreach budget to fund the event, so we all agreed to allow the children's pastor and his team to do this. Our youth pastor and his team, along with several others in our church body, volunteered to help. In the first year, 2,500 people—both children and their parents—came to our Easter egg hunt, and over 400 people responded to the invitation for salvation! Praise God. During the second year, there was a big rainstorm, but about 1,000 people turned up in the pouring rain, and over 200 accepted the Lord. The third year we held this event, we had to move to the rodeo grounds because we had sold our church property. Over 4,000 people came to the Easter egg hunt (in a town of 5,000 and a county of 60,000), and over 500 people responded to the invitation for salvation! The wisdom that brought these souls into the kingdom came through a leader in our church who simply asked the Lord for a Great Commission vision for our community. God will do the same for you! As I mentioned earlier, *he that has a heart to win souls will access the wisdom of God* (Prov. 11:30).

If you remember, our primary target for outreach was to reach the children and youth in our community. The Lord impressed upon me that we needed to invest in young people when they could do nothing for us and eventually they would return that investment by committing to the Lord and His kingdom. We invested hundreds of thousands of dollars into our young people and the youth in our community over the twenty-four years I served as pastor in that church in Decatur. We spent $600,000 on a building designed, decorated, and furnished just for them. We hired a youth pastor to lead and disciple our youth. We sent hundreds of young people on short-term mission trips. We hosted Christian music concerts, youth events like Fifth Quarter (a Friday night after-the-game hangout), special youth speakers, and youth retreats. One Halloween, we even arranged to block off the town square and invited both middle school and high school students to come to a worship and activities night. Scores of young people turned out. The police chief told us that as a result of hosting that event, there was not one instance of vandalism that Halloween.

Several years after I left this church to fulfill a new assignment with Charis Bible College and Andrew Wommack Ministries, we went back to Decatur, Texas to visit family and friends. While we were eating lunch at our favorite Italian restaurant, a young man in his thirties came and stood over our table. With tears in his eyes, he said, "Pastor Greg, you may not remember me, but I was a part of your youth group when I was a teenager. My parents didn't attend your church, but I came often." He went on to say,

"I learned the Word of God while I was there and gave my life to Jesus. Now three of my friends who also came to that youth group and I are each in full-time ministry. We are serving the Lord because you invested in us when we couldn't do anything for you. I just wanted to say thank you for your investment in us and the next generation."

My wife and I were overwhelmed. I did remember him, but I had no idea he had received the Lord, become a disciple of Jesus, and received a call from God while in our youth ministry. That thank-you was worth all the time, money, and investment we made into those young people. With tears of joy streaming down our faces, we thanked God for that divine appointment. He was living proof that all the years we invested in the young people of Decatur made a difference, just as the Lord had spoken to us!

The Word of God says, "*Wisdom is justified by all her children*" (Luke 7:35). You can see the fruit of wisdom in the next generation of your disciples. Wisdom builds generationally. It bears much fruit and makes many disciples. Brothers and sisters, let me encourage and challenge you: If your vision can be fulfilled in your lifetime, it is too small! Where are your disciples? Are you intentionally investing in someone else's life? Are you training someone else to do what you are doing? Are you allowing them to get involved with the joy and fulfillment of your life, ministry, or career? These are not questions intended to bring you guilt or condemnation. Rather, they are intended to challenge you to use the gifts, talents, skill, experience, and influence you have to invest in others. Use the gifts and influence God has given you to win souls and make disciples.

> If your vision can be fulfilled in your lifetime, it is too small!

As you do, you will discover another dimension of God's wisdom made available to you.

I trust the principles I have shared with you in *Walking in Wisdom* have encouraged, inspired, and empowered you to access God's wisdom and the mind of Christ you already possess in your spirit as a born-again child of God. I pray that the spirit of wisdom and revelation in the knowledge of Jesus be released in you today. Declare with me, "I have the mind of Christ. He has been made wisdom unto me in the same way He has been made righteousness unto me. Therefore, I am righteous and I am wise. I make good decisions that line up with the Word of God. I walk in the fear of the Lord and follow the love of God. I listen to godly counsel and surround myself with good friends. I live in God's peace and stay filled with the Spirit. I remain humble and teachable, willing to receive correction. And I possess a vision to win souls and make disciples! The wisdom of God is unlocked and released in me now, in Jesus' name!"

Four Additional Life-Changing Books
by Greg Mohr

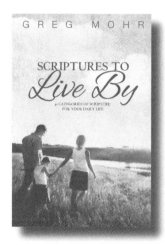

In his best-selling book, *Scriptures to Live By*, Greg Mohr has compiled an arsenal of scriptures in forty-one essential categories that will arm you to face life's difficulties successfully. This book is a tremendous resource for counseling, Bible study, personal reference, and dealing with life's greatest needs.

"Man shall not live by bread alone... but by every Word of God" (Luke 4:4).

Are you or someone you love suffering with a chronic illness? Has someone you know been diagnosed with a terminal disease?

Have you become "sidelined" from healing ministry because you prayed for someone and they failed to improve?

In Greg Mohr's book, *Your Healing Door*, you will discover a number of biblical keys that will unlock healing for your life. Hope and encouragement await you within the pages of this book!

According to 3 John 2, our financial prosperity and physical health are directly linked to the prosperity of our soul.

This revelation leads to an important question: "What constitutes a prosperous soul?"

In *A Prosperous Soul*, Greg Mohr shares the essential keys to establishing a prosperous soul and a healthy, prosperous life.

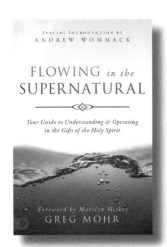

In his book *Flowing in the Supernatural*, Greg offers practical instruction and liberating guidance for operating in the gifts of the Spirit, according to their biblical order. Then we can confidently partner with God to release His supernatural power!

For these resources and other materials, visit **gregmohr.com**.